Thrifty & Thriving

Editing Services: Ann Karako http://www.annieandeverything.com

Publishing and Design Services: MelindaMartin.me

Thrifty & Thriving

More Life For Less Money

Victoria Huizinga

Contents

My Thrifty Life Story

I grew up in a thrifty home. I wore hand-me-downs, ate meals cooked from scratch, picked garden-fresh vegetables as a summer chore, gathered eggs from our own chickens, and was chauffeured around in the same vehicle from the time I was approximately five years old until I was sixteen.

When I started earning my own money and began to realize just how difficult it was, I adopted the thrifty practices of my mother. I was going to make sure that my money would work as hard for me as I did for it.

By the time I graduated high school, I had enough saved to pay for my first year of college. My plan was to work part-time while I went to school full-time and hopefully finish school with very little, if any, student loan debt.

One week into college I met my husband, and a month later we started dating. I quickly realized I couldn't maintain a full-time course load, a part-time job, and a boyfriend; so I ditched the part-time job. Not the best financial decision, I know, but young love can make you do crazy things.

I still worked summers. One summer I even worked two jobs; but in spite of my thrifty practices, they weren't enough to cover my school bills. So I did sign up for more student loans than I originally intended.

Fast forward a few years to when my boyfriend became my husband; and within weeks of the wedding, child number one was on the way. I knew with all my heart that I wanted to be an at-home mom.

To make that work with our budget, my husband and I had to make sacrifices. We were not only paying off student loans left from our dating years, we also had payments from a few not-so-smart purchasing decisions made as a young, married couple. These were going to make living on one income pretty tight.

That is when I stopped being what I would call casually thrifty and instead became a thrifty ninja. I kept tabs on the items we bought, finding the absolute lowest price source for each and every one. Much to my cable-loving husband's chagrin, we cut the cable cord. We cut way back on eating out, to the point that our kids considered Wendy's and Hardee's to be fancy restaurants. We got out from under a truck lease by buying a $250 car, because it was as much cash as we could scrape together at the time.

Now we have one fully-grown child and two teenagers. We are 100% debt free — including the house — and own several rentals. I work at home as the owner of *Snail Pace Transformations*, an online blog. We have more wiggle room financially than we did in the baby years, but we still live like thrifty ninjas — although perhaps not as black belt thrifty ninjas.

We still don't have cable, but we do pay for *Netflix*. I no longer keep tabs on the lowest price source for each and every item we buy, just the dozen or so we buy most often. We do drive used vehicles, but we paid much more than $250 for them.

THRIFTY, FOR US, ISN'T JUST CHOOSING WHETHER OR NOT TO USE A COUPON; IT IS A LIFESTYLE CHOICE.

Along the thrifty life journey I have noticed something: my husband and I have begun to think differently than many of our friends, co-workers, church family, and other people we come into contact with.

Our family has discovered thrifty life principles that guide each and every financial decision we make. Thrifty, for us, isn't just choosing whether or not to use a coupon; it is a lifestyle choice. It means we believe in stewarding our money, possessions, and time well.

Thrifty oozes into how we travel, how we eat, the places we go, the homes we buy, and the stores we frequent.

We are not cheap; we are actually both giving in nature, and being thrifty has rewarded us with opportunities to give in fun and big ways.

Oh, we still worry about money now and again — after all, we are human — but we no longer even desire to spend money without thought. Thrifty living has made us purposeful spenders, and that has allowed us to live a financially free life. Free of debt, free to decide what we want to spend our money on, and free to help those we desire to help.

In the pages of this book I have poured out all my thrifty secrets so that you and your family can become financially free as well. I hope your journey to the thrifty lifestyle is as rewarding as ours has been.

INTRODUCTION

We all know that thrifty family, the one that manages to live on a cash budget with ease. They seem to be able to smell out the freshly marked-down clearance rack like a hunting dog detects a fox. They don't worry about their credit card bill, because there isn't one.

They seem to wear what you wear, eat what you eat, and even earn what you earn, or perhaps they earn even less. Yet they seem to be free of the financial worries that are causing you hours of anxiety each month.

How do they do it? This book is going to show you all their secrets. This is not your typical "how to save money" book. I am not going to list 25 ways to spend less on food or 10 ways to trim down your electric bill. Instead I am going to share key thrifty principles and practices that either come naturally or have been learned over time and practiced so often that they are solid habits now.

Perhaps you already consider yourself a thrifty person. If you truly are, you are still going to find this book helpful; because one of the key personality traits of a thrifty person is their joy in reading every thrifty book they can get their hands on, just to see if they can learn one more tip about saving money that can work for their lives!

How to Use This Book

This book is divided into three sections: "Thrifty People Are," "Thrifty People Do," and "Thrifty People Know."

In "Thrifty People Are," you will learn about some key personality traits I have noticed in myself, my husband, my thrifty friends, and thrifty bloggers and book writers. There is no scientific data to back up my observations; they are just that — observations.

In "Thrifty People Do," you will learn about key things thrifty people do in their lives to keep their expenses as low as possible.

In "Thrifty People Know," you will get a peek into thrifty ninja skills. This chapter is full of ways thrifty people combine money-saving practices to save the most money possible on all their purchases.

By the time you have finished this book, you will have read about more than 40 key thrifty practices and principles. I certainly do not expect you to apply all 40-plus practices and principles to your life tomorrow. This is not a "How To Become A Thrifty Ninja in Only 30 Days" book.

That is why I have given you a snail-pacing action step at the bottom of each chapter, and for many chapters I have also made printable sheets to help guide you in your journey. These are available in my Thrifty & Thriving Printable Pack — yours free when you subscribe to my email list. You can subscribe by visiting the resource page for this book at http://snailpacetranformations.com/thrifty-resources/.

If you have read my blog, *Snail Pace Transformations*, before, you probably know I am a big fan of taking small, snail-pacing steps in every area of life. I believe that gradual change sticks better than sweeping change. I am not a fan of 30-day challenges; they overwhelm me. Because of that, I am not asking you to change your life in a short amount of time, either — I simply want you to agree to start changing your financial practices for the better one small, snail-pacing step at a time.

I heard recently that it takes 90 days for something to become an ingrained habit, not the 21 days most commonly mentioned in the media. I want you to read this book and pick one key thrifty practice that could make the biggest difference to your family's finances — and then stick to it for 90 days. Then pick another and apply it. Continue in this manner, and over time you are going to see a significant change in your finances — one that will last!

SECTION ONE:

Thrifty People Are

Thrifty People Are
NOT PERFECT

My thrifty family is not perfect at handling our money. Yes, you read that right; the author of a book on all things thrifty is saying she isn't a perfect thrifty person.

Some of our family's thrifty mistakes have been small, but some have been huge — as in thousands of dollars wasted.

Why am I admitting to this when it seems like it degrades the value of my thrifty advice? It is because I want you to know that if you make a thrifty mistake too, it is okay. Simply dust yourself off, figure out where you went wrong and what you can do to avoid the mistake the next time, and take the next thrifty step.

When we bought our first renovation home with cash, we got a wee bit caught up in the low price tag of just under $10,000 and neglected to look at one major problem — the ugly, run-down home next to us.

We believed a rumor that it was in the process of being condemned and would soon be taken down by the city. However, after we moved into our new home, we learned the rumor was untrue; and a renter moved in.

When a realtor came to assess the value of our home (one time when we did think briefly about selling it), he told us right away that the ugly, run-down home reduced the value of our fully renovated home significantly. So much, in fact, that when we do finally sell — unless the eyesore next to us is gone — we will be lucky to get as much out of our home as we put into both the purchase and renovations.

More than likely we will face a loss that will cost us thousands of dollars that could have been avoided if we had just researched whether or not there was truth in the rumor.

Since then we have gone on to buy two more homes that we rent out, and the first thing we did both times was to look closely at the conditions of the homes all around the one we were considering buying.

So if you are reading this book and thinking to yourself, "I can't lower my expenses. After all, I can't even figure out how to stack coupons," know that although I can stack coupons, I am not a perfectly thrifty person either. And that is okay; we will learn both from our own mistakes and from those of others who are brave enough to share theirs with us so we can avoid them.

Snail-Pacing Action Step

Starting today, stop beating yourself up about every mistake you make that costs your family money. Instead, praise yourself when you do something right — even if it is as little as remembering to take those coupons to the store with you.

When you do a thrifty action, give yourself a mental high five. A silent, "Yes! Look at how much I just saved!" And when you mess up, say, "How can I learn from this mistake?"

Thrifty People Are
GIVERS

Never confuse a thrifty person with a cheap miser. Sure, thrifty people will probably take home the travel-size bottles of shampoo and soap from the hotel, but we are not going to fill our pockets with sugar packets at the restaurant just so we can use them at home.

A cheap miser is going to exploit every possible trick to save money on their restaurant purchase and then tip the waitress 50 cents. A thrifty person is going to use those same tactics to reduce the cost of their meal, but they are going to tip the waitress at least 20% — and that will be based on the price of the food and drinks before coupons; because they believe that they saved so much money that they can afford to give some of it to the one that has been serving them.

A few years into our marriage, my husband and I met a couple through church that set a limit on their earnings. It wasn't the type of limit that said, "We're willing to earn this much, and when we get there we will stop pursuing more work." Instead it was, "We are willing to run our household on up to this much per month, and when we start earning more than that we will give it all away."

Now, these people tithed from day one of their marriage, even when they were earning less than their give-it-away target, and their target did let them live a comfortable lifestyle; but their vow had a serious impact on my heart.

And they are not the only couple I have observed doing amazing giving with their financial blessings. One of my favorite bloggers is Crystal Paine of *Money Saving Mom.* I started following her back when she had just had her first baby, and now she has three children; I believe the oldest is 10 years old.

I have loved watching her blog grow into one of the largest blogs in North America, and I have cheered more over her successes than she knows. But the one thing that I have noticed about her family is that they give a lot of what they earn away.

Crystal wrote a book called *Money Making Mom,* and my favorite chapter in the entire book has nothing to do with earning money. Instead it is about giving money.

Sure, when our income is little and our expenses are large, it is hard to give in a big way; but we can still give in small ways. We can give of our talents and time and have it not cost us a cent.

We can also lend out our possessions at no cost to our budget. Our family doesn't mind sharing the thrifty purchases we have been blessed with. My husband lends out his tools. I lend out my books earned through *Tyndale Rewards* or bought at yard sales, or I often just give them away with the promise from the receiver that they will pass on the blessing after they are finished.

AS OUR INCOMES GROW, HOWEVER, I THINK EVERY THRIFTY FAMILY NEEDS TO ASK THEMSELVES WHEN ENOUGH IS ENOUGH.

The truth is most of us probably already have enough to live a fairly nice lifestyle compared to the rest of the world. How really necessary is it to increase our standard of living? And what is the cost to others when that is what we continually do with our pay raises?

I am not saying every family should live in a tiny house and own just four outfits each and never eat out so that they can live on little and give big. I am simply saying that after debts are paid, thrifty living loses its purpose for many — but to the truly thrifty, that is when being thrifty just begins to gain its purpose.

Because that is when thrifty families begin to see that their thrifty living lifestyles can make a difference not just in their own lives but in the lives of others. There is just something about helping others that gives life further purpose.

Snail-Pacing Action Step

Spend some time reflecting on what your family's "enough" level is. If reaching that level seems too far away, then instead list ways that you can give to others that won't really cost you all that much money, and begin doing one thing on that list.

Further Resources

Over the past few years I have read key books that have stretched my thinking about just how high I really need to raise my lifestyle to feel fulfilled and how that affects my ability to give to those in great need.

You can see this list of books by visiting the resource page for this book, which is found on my blog, *Snail Pace Transformations,* at http://snailpacetransformations.com/thrifty-resources/.

Thrifty People Are

Uniquely Thrifty

A thrifty person can spend hours comparing prices, but they try not to waste any time on comparing their thrifty to someone else's thrifty. Thrifty people might be intrigued by another person's thrifty life, but they are not going to expend effort feeling like they don't measure up.

Why? Because a thrifty lifestyle is almost impossible to compare. Every thrifty family has their own thrifty "why." A family's thrifty why is going to determine their priorities, and these priorities are as unique as the individual. (You will learn more about the importance of having a thrifty why in the chapter "Thrifty People Are Goal-Focused.")

Perhaps one family wants to get out of debt. So they lower expenses in every way possible for a set amount of time until all the debts are paid. Once the debts are gone, they have more money to work with, so they add in things that they truly missed during the paying-off-debt period.

Are the things they add in thrifty? Yes, they can be, as long as they fit within the three elements of a thrifty splurge.

Three Elements of a Thrifty Splurge

Thrifty splurges fit in a cash-only budget. Thrifty people are not going to go into debt for a splurge. They are going to go without, unless they can afford to pay for it in cash.

Thrifty splurges do not significantly slow the pace of reaching large financial goals. Thrifty people know that life can get pretty boring if all they are doing is saving money to reach that next big financial goal. So instead of throwing all their money at one big financial target, they allow a small percentage of their money to go to splurges. This decision does slow down their ability to reach their big financial goals, but the trade-off can be significantly positive.

Relationship-building splurges are worth slowing down your financial goals for.

For instance, perhaps your family is saving up for a new-to-you car. You know that it will take two years if you throw everything you can at the car fund — but your son graduates in one year, and you really like the sound of one last family vacation before he leaves the nest.

You work the numbers and realize you can afford BOTH a car and a vacation if you are willing to compromise. So you book a place with a kitchen so you can save money by eating in during vacation, and you wait six months longer for the new-to-you car.

Your family goes for it and has memories for years to come of that family vacation. And you can barely remember driving the rust bucket six extra months to make it happen.

Relationship-building splurges are worth slowing down your financial goals for.

Thrifty splurges bring you joy either short-term or long-term. A short-term splurge is usually something that lasts a small amount of time, like a cup of coffee from your favorite coffee shop on a day you needed a pick-me-up; or it can be a week-long vacation as a family.

A long-term splurge is an investment in a piece of equipment that can be used to build memories, such as a backyard pool, trampoline, outdoor theatre, or whatever your thrifty family is into doing together.

Both types of splurges bring you joy. Both types of splurges can build fond memories.

Thrifty living does not mean that you cut your life down to just the essentials. Thrifty living means you get to decide where your money is going to go, and you make every penny stretch as far as possible — so you can add more into your budget for less money.

DECIDING WHERE TO SPLURGE AND WHERE TO SAVE IS UP TO YOUR THRIFTY FAMILY

The beauty of being thrifty is that you get to decide which areas to cut, because you are in control of your money and not the other way around.

Keep your grocery budget to a minimum but splurge on that $50 gourmet pizza joint once a week, if you can pay cash and not go into debt for it. Cut your hair at home but buy $100 jeans, if you can do it without flashing the credit card. The thrifty lifestyle is all about priorities and balancing the checkbook.

Of course, some decisions run deeper than choosing to color your hair at home over having it done in a salon so that you can afford those designer jeans. In our family, we have chosen to have my husband home more. On our income, that has meant choosing to live in a neighborhood that is far from the nicest in our town so that we could be debt-free and also investing a good portion of our unexpected windfalls (more on those in the chapter "Thrifty People Do Use Windfalls Wisely") into two rentals which provide another income stream.

The combined effect from the amount of money we save by not having a mortgage to pay each month and the income from the two rentals has not only allowed my husband to work less; it has also allowed us to do some pretty fun memory-making adventures, too.

Sure, there are days where we get tempted to take out a small mortgage and move to a nicer neighborhood, perhaps with a few acres of land. But then we run the numbers and realize that if we did, we would have to give up the money we spend on family "daycations," camping, and other family fun. With our children being home just a few short years more, these are not cuts we want to make right now .

The thrifty lifestyle is all about choices — not about keeping every expense to a minimum. Being thrifty simply means that you get to decide which priorities make it into your cash budget and which don't.

Thrifty people and their thrifty families are not going to judge your financial priorities against their own. Thriftiness is as unique as the person who is practicing it.

Thrifty people only care about one thing: are you being a wise steward of the finances you have been given, making sure that they are handled in a way that brings you and those you love joy, without the unnecessary burden of stress so many of us add?

Snail-Pacing Action Step

Take a few moments this week to sit down with a pad of paper and write down your thrifty purchases that others might view as completely unnecessary. Include everything from the excess of clothing in your closet to the *Netflix* account. This can be really eye-opening and cause us to remember that living the thrifty lifestyle isn't about winning the prize for keeping our expenses as low as possible but about keeping our expenses within our cash means — yet not at the cost of our long-term financial dreams.

Thrifty People Are
Budget-Makers

Thrifty people live within their means, taking on very little to no debt. I think most thrifty people would agree that all debt, including your home mortgage, should never equal more than 25% percent of your take-home pay. I also think most thrifty people would say less debt than that, or no debt at all, is even better.

To keep low debt to no debt, a thrifty person uses the power of a budget to keep them from overspending. A budget allows a thrifty family to know exactly what is coming in and what is going out of their bank accounts. It helps them to manage every penny well and acts as a guide for what they can and can't afford.

Before a thrifty person takes on a new ongoing expense (like ballet lessons for their child), they are going to check their budget to see if the expense will fit. If it doesn't fit, they will review their budget again to see what they could give up to make it fit. If there is nothing to give up, they will figure out if they can grow their income to fit it in. If they brainstorm all three of these and come up empty-handed, they simply won't take on the added ongoing expense.

So how do thrifty people budget? Well, each thrifty family varies in their budgeting style.

Our family has a set, month-to-month budget of expenses that never change, as well as a list of upcoming non-regular expenses that we will need to pay soon.

Regular expenses include utilities, food, insurance, medications, payments to our car replacement fund, and a few other items. These expenses equal my husband's base take-home pay.

Non-regular expenses vary throughout the year. To fund those we use my husband's overtime pay, his second job pay, bonuses, third checks (we get paid every other week, so two times a year we get three checks in a month), rental income, and income from my blog.

Our budget is constantly changing. I retype the monthly set budget at least once a quarter due to either gas prices going up or down, food prices going up or down, or an expense being added in or taken out.

As for non-regular expenses, I try to look at least three months in advance and plan for what I do know. I write down things like upcoming birthdays, trips we want to take, and projects we want to do and their totals; and then I start knocking these items off the list as I can.

We keep a $1,000 short-term emergency fund in our checking account for things we can't predict, like the car needing a repair or a member of our family requiring medical attention.

Keeping this short-term emergency fund fully topped up takes priority over any non-regular expenses that are more wants than needs. (There is more information on this fund and how it works in the chapter "Thrifty People Are Big Believers in the Unexpected.")

There really is no wrong or right way to write a budget, in my opinion, just as long as it keeps you living within your means.

For instance, we prefer paper and pen for our record keeping, but I know plenty of thrifty families who rave about budget software and apps such as *You Need A Budget*, *Mvelopes* and Dave Ramsey's budget app, *Every Dollar*. The key is to find what method of budgeting works for your family and keep using it.

Snail-Pacing Action Step

If your family has never set up a budget before, you need to take action and create one. Go to Dave Ramsey's website or the *Crown Financial Ministries* website for help on how to create a budget that works.

If you have a budget but it just doesn't seem to be working, revisit it and brainstorm why it isn't effective. It might just be that the style of budget you are using isn't a good fit. If you are using pen and paper, try a smartphone app budget or vice versa. Never give up on budgeting! It is a vital tool to financial success.

Further Resources

For a list of my favorite websites and books for budgeting assistance, visit the resource page for this book at http://snailpacetransformations.com/thrifty-resources/.

Thrifty People Are
BIG BELIEVERS IN THE UNEXPECTED

I think the most frustrating thing for people trying to live on a budget for the first time is all the unexpected bills that come in. Newbie budgeters fill in those neat little areas in the free budget printables they downloaded and printed, and wham! Something not on one of the lines comes up.

Thrifty people expect unexpected expenses. Oh, they still get frustrated with them, but they don't stress about them as much as they once did; because thrifty people have a backup plan.

In our thrifty family we have a three-step backup plan that helps us prepare for the unexpected, stay out of debt, and continue on an all-cash budget.

THE SLUSH FUND

A slush fund is an amount of money set aside that covers the small stuff that pops up. It could be tiny emergencies like the $10 to $30 copay to see the doctor (the big bill comes later and is paid from another fund).

It can pay for spontaneous, fun events that we just don't want to say no to, like a dinner out with friends who came into town unannounced.

Generally our family funds this slush fund by leaving around $50 in our bank account that isn't claimed for any other bill purposes.

Since our family is truly thrifty at heart, we are not tempted to spend that $50 week in and week out. Sometimes it takes weeks before it will be spent, sometimes it is gone the day after we put it there. When it is gone, it is gone; and then we say no to everything we can.

The Small Emergency Fund

Our small emergency fund is our second wall against letting the unexpected keep us from staying on a cash budget.

Basically the small emergency fund is how we plan for what we'll call the semi-unexpected. We know cars will need repairs, but we don't know when or what the repairs will cost. We know the kids will need dental check-ups, but we don't know what surprises the dentist will find or the amount we'll have to pay for them.

In the last chapter I covered how we maintain our small emergency fund at $1000.

Currently, our cars and household appliances are getting older, though, so we think we might increase this small emergency fund to $1500 to $2000, as repairs on our vehicles and the need to replace our large household appliances are both becoming more likely.

The most helpful part of our short-term emergency fund is that it makes living on a cash budget much more possible and decreases stress. The small emergency fund is truly essential if you want to start controlling your finances instead of having them control you.

The short-term emergency fund is in our everyday checking account. If this kind of accessibility is too much temptation for you, then put it in a separate account; but make it possible to transfer funds online if needed. That one extra step should be enough to cause you to think twice about whether what you want the money for is a true emergency or not.

The reason why our thrifty family thinks the short-term emergency fund needs to be readily available is that emergencies don't happen just during banking hours. Tires pop early Saturday morning. Washing machines decide they don't want to wash their last load at 7pm the night before your family vacation, when you thought you could plan on doing all the laundry you would need for the trip.

If the money is readily available, you can take care of the emergencies with a debit card right away, without needing to put it on a credit card. Yes putting it on a credit card is doable, especially since you do have the cash saved, but many thrifty people prefer living without a credit card. The pros and cons of credit cards are lengthy, so I won't go into them here; but I will say that in our thrifty family we prefer to not use credit cards.

Sometimes our short-term emergency fund stays fully funded for months; other times it gets hit week after week, and it takes us awhile to get it back up to $1000.

The Long-Term Emergency Fund

I have heard experts say that you should have a long-term emergency fund worth anywhere from three months to as many as 12 months of your take-home income. For our thrifty family, our long-term emergency fund is currently equal to what we could squeeze by on for three months.

Our thrifty family makes the long-term fund much harder to get to than the short-term emergency fund. It is kept at an entirely different bank than our everyday bank account. It has no debit card attached to it. It is not set up for online banking. We don't have a checkbook for it. We literally have to go in during banking hours to get the cash out.

The long-term emergency fund never gets touched unless something huge happens, such as a job loss, large medical emergency, or significant unforeseen house repair that becomes needed (i.e., something not fully covered by homeowners insurance).

Snail-Pacing Action Step

If you don't have any of these types of funds, I suggest you start first with creating a slush fund. Set aside a small amount of money from each paycheck for incidentals that come up.

After you have established that small slush fund, quickly move on to creating your small emergency fund of $1,000 to $2,000 dollars, depending on how old your vehicles and major appliances are. You notice I said "quickly," a word I don't use often. I used it because I believe out of all three funds mentioned, having the small emergency fund is the most vital to helping you get out of debt and stay out. All three funds are needed and important, but the middle one is a game-changer.

Further Resources

I have included a list of ways to raise money to build your $1000 emergency fund in the resources section for this book, which is found on my blog, *Snail Pace*

Transformations, at http://snailpacetransformations. com/thrifty-resources/.

Thrifty People Are
PLANNERS

Thrifty people know that spending a few minutes each month to think ahead to the expenses that are going to pop up in the next few weeks, the next few months, and even up to the next year can save more money than most people might think.

HOW PLANNING CAN SAVE YOU MONEY

When you think ahead about what you need, you have time to find the most inexpensive source for it.

A good everyday example of this is our family's "gift tote." I keep it stashed with items I find anywhere from 50% to sometimes as high as 90% off. When a gift is needed, I can shop my "gift tote" instead of making a last minute trip to the store to purchase something at full price, which would waste both money and time.

A Few Places To Find Inexpensive Items Before You Need Them

Yard Sales: Thrifty people take inventory before yard sale season begins. What new furniture pieces would be nice to add to the home, or which ones need to be replaced? What clothing needs do family members have?

Clearance Sales: There is an entire chapter later in the book explaining how thrifty people view holiday clearance in a very unique way; but, of course, holiday clearance aisles are not the only type of clearance sales thrifty people hit.

For instance, at the end of summer I personally take note of what summer supplies we will need for next summer and search clearance sales for them. Will we need new pool toys? Swimsuits? Swim goggles? Are our beach towels going to hold up for one more year?

Discount Gift Cards: Thrifty people also use the think-ahead principle when buying discounted gift cards from sites like Cardpool. (See the chapter "Thrifty People Know Gift Cards Are Not Just for Gift-Giving" for more details.)

Do we plan to see a movie as a family soon? If yes, then I will buy a discounted gift card for our local movie theater chain and save as much as 20 percent before we even walk in the door.

Grocery Store Sales: Thinking ahead can also be applied to groceries. If you know your family uses ketchup at an alarming rate (or is that just our family?)

then it makes sense to buy enough for two or three months when you see a great sale on it.

Early Bird Specials For Events: Early bird specials are also available to those who think ahead. I love to run, and if I pay my race entry fees months before the race, I get a special early-bird discount that can be as much as $20 off one race. These specials are also found for conferences and other events.

Thinking ahead is not only a great money-saver; it is a great stress-reliever. Events and seasonal needs have a way of sneaking up on us; but when you shop ahead, you have what you need when you need it, at a much smaller price tag.

SNAIL-PACING ACTION STEP

Pick the one area from the list above where you think you could save your family the most money and start making thinking ahead a habit in that area. Once that habit is formed, try doing it with another area from the list.

Further Resources

I have included a list of my family's favorite places to get online discounts on the resource page for this book at http://snailpacetransformations.com/thrifty-resources/.

Thrifty People Are
GOAL-FOCUSED

Let's face it: keeping your expenses to a minimum is hard work. It is a lot easier and a lot less time-consuming to drive to the closest store, throw what you need in the cart, drive home, and use it, than to take time to think about whether you really need it, try to borrow it, wait for a sale, price check, and then perhaps, maybe, buy it.

However, the first process is going to cost you a lot more money than the second, and that means your money won't go as far as it could.

In order to make the effort of keeping your expenses low worth it, you have to know your "why." Why are you wanting to lower your expenses?

For our family it started off with a desire to give our children the benefit that an at-home parent can provide. Now, we have seen plenty of families with two working parents who do a wonderful job of balancing it all, but we knew that wasn't what we wanted for our family.

YOUR FAMILY'S THRIFTY WHY

It doesn't have to be as long-term as keeping one parent home during the years the children are home. It can be more short-term. In fact, I think you need a mix of both long-term and short-term goals to really keep focused.

Perhaps your long-term why is to have a fully-funded college fund to give your children the gift of a debt-free start in life.

Your short-term why could be saving up for a family vacation, or putting aside enough cash for a better family car.

SNAIL-PACING ACTION STEP

Sit down and think about your thrifty why, both long- and short-term. If you have a spouse, make sure to discuss this together.

FURTHER RESOURCES

For a list of my favorite books on goal-setting, check out the resource page for this book at http://snailpacetransformations.com/thrifty-resources/.

Thrifty People Are
Cash Buyers

Thrifty people pay cash for items big and small. Thrifty people know that there are many benefits to paying with cash.

Paying cash makes you more aware of what you are paying

For a period of about one year in our marriage we tried using one of those point rewards credit cards. We thought we could keep track of all of our expenses all month long, not spending more than we earned, and reaping the added benefits of a points card.

Let me just say that it is so easy to quickly lose track of what you're spending when money isn't coming directly out of your account. When I pay with a debit card I am constantly keeping track, because I want to make sure that my account does not become overdrawn. When I pay with cash, I can't spend more than what I have, period. But when I pay with a credit card, for some reason that same sense of urgency to tally up my purchases flies out the window. Then when the bill comes in I am faced with too many purchases and not enough cash to cover them.

At least, that used to be the case. My husband and I soon learned the error of our ways and switched to cash or debit purchases only (with rare exceptions) early in our marriage.

When you spend cash, it is automatically gone. You can't overspend.

Paying cash avoids interest payments

Earlier in our marriage we took car loans out on several vehicles. When the time came to sign the loan agreements, I would always make myself read the interest costs, just to inspire myself a bit more to pay the loan off early. That line showing the total interest was always shocking. It certainly took a huge bite out of the "sweet deal" the car dealer said we were getting. Interest is not thrifty — period!

Paying cash often gets you a deal

One way we save every week by paying cash is at the gas pump. A certain gas station in our area takes off five cents a gallon if you pay cash. That small discount might not seem like much, but I figured out that I save, on average, 80 cents per fill up. I fill up my SUV usually once a week. Since there are 52 weeks in a year, that means that tiny 5-cent-per-gallon discount saves me $41.60 every year.

$42 might not seem like much, but this is just one example of a discount our family receives for paying cash. There are many more cash purchases that save our family money in little ways, and all of them together add up to big savings year after year.

Paying Cash Forces You To Live According To Your Priorities

Living on a cash-up-front budget has been eye-opening for our family. It forces us to make priorities for our money, since we can only make it stretch so far.

For instance, I remember a certain tight financial month when we needed both a new vacuum and a new pair of shoes for our son. In the end we made the vacuum last a bit longer with a duct tape fix and bought the shoes. To us, shoes for our son were more important than a duct-tape-free vacuum cleaner.

Paying Cash Forces You To Live Within Your Means Or Change Your Means

Living with cash has also made us more realistic about our earnings and just how far we can stretch them.

Yes, we are thrifty, but thrifty can't fix all money woes — you can only take money-saving so far. Sometimes you either just need to create a larger income to live the way you want to live, or let go of your desire to live at a certain lifestyle level. Living on a cash-only budget makes you face this reality daily.

How To Live On Cash For Regular Purchases

Even though I am using the word "cash" in this chapter, I want you to know that our thrifty family doesn't always pay in actual, hold-in-the-hand cash; instead we often use our debit card.

To make sure we don't spend too much in one area, I have a super-simple paper form I fill out for each area of our budget. At the top I write what area of the budget is being kept tabs on, such as "food," and then I have lines for "where," "withdraw," "deposit," and "balance." I regularly update these ledgers so we have an accurate idea of how much we have to spend in each category at all times.

You can grab your own copy of my simple cash budget sheet at http://snailpacetransformations.com/thrifty-resources/ as part of the printable pack that goes with this book.

If you are more digitally inclined than our thrifty family, you might want to check out smartphone financial apps such as *You Need A Budget (YNAB)* or *EveryDollar*. I have heard great things about both apps, and perhaps someday this pen-and-paper gal will take the plunge.

For now our thrifty family sticks to paper ledgers as well as cash envelopes. Currently our cash envelopes are used for gas (because we get a discount for paying cash) and the number one area of our budget that needs a close watch — eating out.

We used to have cash envelopes for several more categories, but over the years our family has begun buying more things online. Obviously you can't pay with cash online, so we found ourselves taking money out of our bank account only to have to put it back in again to cover an online purchase. To fix this problem we simply switched to more paper ledger categories.

Eating out, however, is not something one can do online. And for us, time and time again when we have neglected to use actual cash and have decided to just use the debit card instead, eating out has gone over budget fast.

However, when we have cash in-hand for eating out, we can clearly see when we are out of money and therefore have to go home for dinner.

LIVING ON CASH FOR BIG PURCHASES

We handle saving up for the vast majority of big purchases by ordering them by priority of what needs to be paid for next. For instance, currently on my list are "tickets for hubby to visit family" and "fix truck door." The door is last priority, since it still does open — but only by rolling down the window, which is annoying but doable. However, as it should be, getting my husband to see his out-of-town family is more important to us than fixing a door that essentially still works — so the door fix has been pushed until last.

I talk about how we find money for these big variable expenses more in the chapter "Thrifty People Do Keep A Wish List."

There is really only one exception to this rule, and that is how we save up for cars. When we paid off our last vehicle loan, the second I got off the phone with the loan officer I grabbed my shoes and coat and headed to the bank. I had them set up an automatic transfer from one account to another of an amount equal to a modest car loan payment twice a month (one transfer for each vehicle we own).

This account has become known as our "car replacement fund," although on my budget I never changed the wording; so it still says "car payment." Personally, I like it that way, because it helps me forget about the money I send to that account each month. My brain seems to think it is still going to the car loan people and isn't mine to touch.

Essentially we pay a car payment to ourselves but with one huge difference — ours is interest free.

Snail-Pacing Action Point

Start paying for at least one area of your budget with cash this month. A good place to start is in whatever area of your budget is the most out of control. At the beginning of the week, take out what you have budgeted to spend that week in that area; and when it is gone, don't touch your debit card (or worse, your credit cards) to continue spending in this area. Instead just do without.

Thrifty People Are
Good at Time Management

Thrifty people know that time equals money. The better that time is spent, the more money that can be made or saved.

This isn't to say that thrifty families are all work and no play. My family enjoys camping, kayaking, at-home movie nights, and many other relationship-building activities that have nothing to do with saving or earning money — except for the fact that we approach them in a thrifty way, spending the least amount of money possible on them.

What I mean is that thrifty people manage their time well so that they can get the maximum return on their investment, just like they do with their money.

This chapter is just going to scratch the surface of all that goes into managing your time well. Time management is a topic that truly should be explained with more than one chapter, so make sure to check out my resources at the end of this chapter for books I love on the topic and other articles I have written on it.

For this chapter, I am going to give you three key ways that I manage my time that allow me to take charge of my day and get more done.

I am going to keep things personal in this chapter, because I know all thrifty families are unique, and what they do to manage their time well is going to differ from what I do.

I KEEP A TO-DO LIST

My to-do list is not complicated. Currently, it is the top piece of paper on a clipboard full of one-sided printer paper (I am thrifty & green, remember? No way am I recycling that paper until both sides are used).

I draw a line horizontally across the middle of the paper and write "blog" on the top half and "home" on the bottom half. I write everything I would like to get done in the next few days on that list. Then I circle any appointments for the current day, and I place a star near the top three things I need to get done.

I get those three things done first and work on the rest as I can. The next day I rewrite the list and pick another three things.

I AM RARELY EMPTY-HANDED

My knitting, a book, a full podcast line-up on my phone, and of course my smartphone go wherever I go. I use these items during waiting times and other little moments to get a lot done.

For instance, if my husband is driving, I am knitting; and my knitting (thanks to all the ways I know of to keep it a low-cost habit) creates great, low-cost gifts for our family to give to others.

If I am waiting in line, I am deleting emails that I don't even need to read, or liking pins on *Pinterest* so I can read them later and see if they are something I want to add to my boards (for bloggers, *Pinterest* is work). If I am in a waiting room, I will read a book on my *Kindle* app. If I have a long, solo drive ahead of me, I get out my podcasts about how to blog better and start listening the hours away.

I AM ALWAYS TWEAKING

I have an entire chapter on how being a lifetime learner is a key thrifty principle, and this certainly relates to time management. I am constantly re-evaluating what is working for me and what isn't.

Life is in a constant state of motion. What the best use of your time is right now, in this season, might not be so in the next season — which could be just a few months away.

When I start to notice that I am not being as productive with my days as I once was, I begin to look for the reason. Is it me? Am I becoming unfocused? Or is it that my schedule needs to change because something in my life has changed?

For moms who work at home, I think the last question is the answer 9 times out of 10. All it takes for a schedule to stop working is junior signing up for the school play that has multiple practices a week, and that routine that once flowed perfectly is suddenly no longer working.

This is when it is time to call a business meeting with yourself. How do you need to tweak your schedule to to be as productive as you once were before this new event was added?

It might mean packing a bag of items that you can work on during the practice, instead of driving there and back twice to drop your child off and pick him up. This would save on travel time, and if you can manage to not bring another child along, it makes a nice quiet hour or two to get stuff done. It could mean that you find out who else is in the play and see if you could form some type of carpool, so you don't have to drive every time.

This is when thrifty people put on their creative thinking caps and allow their minds to ponder the possibilities of how to best get more done in this new season, without overwhelming themselves or their family.

These three techniques — keeping a to-do list, having things to do handy, and frequently tweaking my routine — are how I am able to make time not just for money-saving and money-earning activities, but also for meaningful relationships with those I love. I save and earn money mostly in the in-between moments of my day, so I can leave the bulk of my time open to serving my family well.

I CONCENTRATE ON THE MUST DO'S AND LET THE SHOULD DO'S SLIDE, SO I CAN KEEP MY MAIN PRIORITY IN LIFE MY MAIN PRIORITY —AND THAT IS LOVING MY FAMILY WELL.

I am not a perfectionist in anything I do so that I have time to enjoy the mess that is life. I am the queen of "good enough." I would rather have a home with a pile of clutter here or there and take the time I save not fussing about perfect decor and spend it on building relationships and restoring myself instead. Life is too short for perfection.

SNAIL-PACING ACTION STEP

Pick one of the three key time management steps I mentioned to work on each day. I also urge you to check out one time management book from your local library.

FURTHER RESOURCES

For a list of books I recommend on time management and articles I have written about it on my blog, *Snail Pace Transformations,* visit http://snailpacetransformations. com/thrifty-resources/.

Thrifty People Are
LIFETIME LEARNERS

Thrifty people are always seeking out new ways to save, and that requires them to have the attitude of lifetime learners. Thrifty people never think to themselves that they are too old to learn something new. Instead they embrace learning new things as an exciting part of life.

Thrifty people make learning a priority in their lives by setting aside other, lesser things. You might find a thrifty person reading while curled up on the couch at night instead of watching TV. Or they will have the TV on, but they will be watching educational shows that teach them new skills.

A thrifty person might try to learn a new skill so that they don't have to hire it out; or they might read a book, a blog, or a magazine that shares thrifty wisdom, just to see if they are missing out on a way to lower their expenses.

Thrifty people of course learn through free sources of information whenever possible. They borrow books from the library. Thrifty people search *iTunes* or *Stitcher* for podcasts on subjects they wish to improve in. Thrifty people also have the *Kindle* app on their smartphone loaded with free titles on topics they desire to learn more about, allowing them to fit in a few minutes of reading here and there throughout the day.

If a book, podcast, or free *YouTube* video doesn't seem to be helping a thrifty person learn what they want to know, they will search out someone in real life to teach them.

A thrifty person will even pay a fee for a course in something if they know that it will help them learn a new skill that will either save or make money in the long run.

Snail-Pacing Action Step

Take a moment to list one new skill that interests you, that you know will also save your family money. Perhaps it is cooking more from scratch, or learning how to do a few basic DIY things around the house. In the next few weeks make it a priority to seek out ways to learn your desired skill.

Further Reading

For more information on how to fit in time for learning, visit the resource page for this book at http://snailpacetransformations.com/thrifty-resources/.

Thrifty People Are
QUESTION-ASKERS

Thrifty people are not afraid of asking, and I am not just talking about the classic thrifty question of asking for a discount.

THRIFTY PEOPLE ASK TO BORROW ITEMS

When my husband and I have a need, we often will put a shout out to our friends to see if anyone has something that might help to fulfill our need. We ask with a heart that is completely willing to return the favor.

For instance, for our son's graduation open house we needed a few coolers to hold drinks and ice. I updated my *Facebook* status with the question "Does anyone have a family-sized cooler we could borrow?" — and within minutes I had three friends willing to lend me a cooler.

Sometimes we will ask around to those friends we see in person, and other times, like the example above, we will send a plea out on *Facebook*.

THRIFTY PEOPLE ASK FOR OPINIONS

When I was looking into purchasing a blender, I asked my *Facebook* friends which type of blender they had and if they were happy with it. I got back a lot of opinions on blenders ranging from $40 to $400, and then I took those suggestions and read reviews on the brands my friends had suggested. I ended up going with the $40 blender, and several years later it is still going strong.

THRIFTY PEOPLE ASK FOR SUGGESTIONS

When a thrifty family wants to eat out somewhere new or explore an attraction they've never been to in the local area, they ask their *Facebook* friends for ideas and thrifty pointers.

Our family has done this for thrifty vacation ideas, too; and we have discovered some great thrifty day trips, just by asking others where they like to go that is relatively inexpensive.

THRIFTY PEOPLE ASK FOR THRIFTY TIPS

No thrifty person or thrifty family is an expert in all things thrifty. Sometimes I find myself making a purchase in a realm I have no experience in. When that happens I reach out to my friends in person and on *Facebook* and ask them how they save money on that particular item.

For instance, I did this when my sons started to need eyeglasses, and I found my friends to be a wealth of thrifty eyeglass shopping information.

THRIFTY PEOPLE DO ASK FOR A DISCOUNT

Yes, I did say that thrifty people ask more questions than the classic "Can I have a discount?" — but I didn't say I wasn't going to talk about this well-known question.

Our thrifty family only asks for discounts at places where we feel it is appropriate, but not as often as you might think; because truthfully we have done all our research before ever entering the store. We know that the store's prices are already awesome, and we feel that alone should be rewarded by our not asking for a further discount. I know that might make some thrifty people gasp in horror, but it is what our family believes and practices.

To us it seems like there are settings where negotiating a price is expected and others where it is just plain rude. We will negotiate prices at the car lot. We will negotiate prices at yard sales. We won't negotiate prices with the local bike shop owner, who doesn't really ask much more for his bikes than department stores and offers routine maintenance on them for either low or no cost. To us the extra money out-of-pocket for the bike is worth the great low-cost service we receive for years to come.

THRIFTY PEOPLE ASK FOR AN IN-PERSON TUTORIAL

Sometimes what a thrifty person needs isn't help in purchasing an item but instruction about how to use or maintain an item they already own.

When I got my DSLR camera for the blog, I asked a friend of mine who takes amazing photos if she could come over and show me how to use it.

When I simply couldn't make sense of the *YouTube* video on how to backwash our above-ground pool pump, I called a friend who had one and asked him if he would be willing to stop by and help me the first time.

Our friends are willing to help us with these things because they know we are willing to help them in return.

SNAIL-PACING ACTION STEP

The next time you find yourself with a question for which the answer could save you money, ask your friends. You might find they are a wealth of thrifty knowledge that is just waiting to be tapped into.

Thrifty People Are
RESEARCHERS

Thrifty people are not known to make spontaneous purchases. Instead, each and every purchase begins with researching the product — but it doesn't stop there.

RESEARCHING THE REVIEWS

Thrifty people will read the reviews on items they want to buy, to check out what others have to say about the item.

They will compare prices from brand to brand, sometimes making the final decision to purchase the more expensive model, because it seems like the reviews are saying it lasts longer.

My personal favorite place to read reviews is *Amazon*, simply because of the vast quantity available. Even if I have no plans to buy that exact item on *Amazon*, I will research it there.

For travel purchases such as hotel rooms, I like *TripAdvisor* for the same reason I like *Amazon*: there are lots of reviews to read. Our thrifty family also likes

TripAdvisor because of the pictures hotel reviewers are allowed to post of the hotel. These pictures give us a better idea of what the hotel really looks like, more than the staged photos on the hotel's website.

For vehicle purchases, our thrifty family loves *Kelley Blue Book*. On numerous occasions it has stopped our family from buying a potential lemon. When we stick to *Kelley Blue Book* recommendations, we have never regretted our vehicle choices.

One last place our thrifty family loves to get reviews from is *Facebook*. Many items that we love have been purchased as a result of a *Facebook* plea for recommendations. We have also had great luck polling *Facebook* friends about vacation locations, restaurants, and more, all with great results.

RESEARCHING THE PRICE

Thrifty people never take the salesman at his word when he claims the price at his store is "the lowest price." Thrifty people, before walking into any store, have done their footwork online to figure out what the lowest price really is.

If the item the thrifty person wants to buy is used, they will check *eBay* and *Craigslist* first to see what the going rate on the secondhand market is before they purchase.

If the item is new, they will check out prices on a few major sites such as *Ebay* and *Amazon*.

Researching how to maintain and fix it

Thrifty people also research what might be done to keep the items they already own lasting longer, as well as how to do DIY minor repairs to these items.

For instance, when two of our ceramic stovetop elements stopped working, our thrifty family didn't pick up the phone to call the repairman. Nope! This thrifty family picked up the iPad instead and started searching for *YouTube* videos on how to repair the stovetop — then hopped over to *Amazon* to order the parts.

Our family has also saved a bundle on maintenance on our above-ground pool by again using the power of *YouTube* and a little help from our friends. Through *YouTube* videos and hands-on instructions from friends who also own above-ground pools, we have learned how to properly open our pool each spring, clean and maintain it all summer long, and close it when fall arrives.

Snail-Pacing Action Step

Next time you realize your family needs an item, take fifteen minutes researching it. Spend five minutes reading reviews, five minutes comparing prices at various websites, and the last five minutes creating a *Facebook* status to poll your friends about the item. Ask them if they own one, and if so what brand? What did they pay for it? Where did they buy it? Are they happy with the item and with the customer service they received there? Would they buy it again? And at the same place?

After you have gathered your research, then sleep on it for 24 hours. Before you buy, ask yourself one last question: "Do we really need this?"

Thrifty People Are
NOT AFRAID OF DIY

Because thrifty people are lifelong learners, they also tend to have a love for DIY-ing.

For our family, *YouTube* has become our go-to site for DIY help. Why? Because of the excellent visual tutorials on how to fix or service items.

Thanks to *YouTube*, my husband was able to figure out how to properly refinish the hardwood floors in a rental of ours. Thanks to *YouTube*, my husband also learned how to correctly edge laminate countertops.

Books explaining how to do things can also be extremely helpful. Books purchased for just $3 each at a *Big Lots* closeout helped us do a lot of renovation work on the home we purchased for $10,000.

Home renovation isn't the only place where approaching things with a DIY attitude can save money. You can save money when you learn how to grow your own food, cook from scratch, make your own cleaning solutions, and much, much more.

Podcasts and blog posts have become a valuable resource to me in learning how to blog effectively. I especially love learning from podcasts, because I can listen to them while working out, or doing chores, or even while working on other DIY projects.

A word of caution: not all DIY projects are cheaper than buying. For instance, a lot of crafts can cost way more in supplies than purchasing ready-made items. You also need to consider the cost of your time.

If you earn a significant amount per hour, taking time to make or fix something yourself may not be worth the return. Instead it might make more sense to work a few more hours and pay someone to do the job.

To figure out if it makes financial sense for you to tackle a DIY job, use half of your take-home hourly wage as a guideline. A DIY project worth doing should save you at least that amount for every hour that you put into it. If it doesn't, then — unless you really enjoy it — leave the job to the professionals or buy the item ready-made.

Why half? Again, that is just a guideline. Sometimes it is nice to do something different than our paid jobs, and also DIY work is for the most part a lot more flexible than paid work. There is also the effort/time spent on finding someone to do certain DIY work.

For our family, if we can save half of what my husband earns in an hour for each hour we are DIY-ing, it is worth it. We find great benefit in the flexibility to do it when we can, the personal satisfaction for doing it ourselves, and the effort saved by not having to find someone else to do it.

If you are retired or the at-home parent, you might be saying, "But I don't have an hourly wage." True, and in that case, do the things that will save you the most money in the time you have available; and spend your money on the things you are not talented at. For our family, that means we keep track of the prices of the food items we buy the most, but we don't rinse out *Ziploc* bags. It also means we spend money on getting our children's hair cut, but we rarely spend money on labor for home renovations.

An added benefit of being willing to learn a new skill to save money is that sometimes you find out you have a natural talent in that new skill, and it can become a way to make money or a way to give to others through the gift of service.

Snail-Pacing Action Step

Choose one thing that you routinely buy that you could save money by DIYing, and then study up on how to do just that. Remember: it takes awhile to become efficient at a new skill. Don't stop after your first try just because it was a flop. Learn from your mistakes and slowly, over time, you will get better and start saving money by DIYing instead of buying.

Thrifty People Are
Out-Of-The-Box Thinkers

Out of all the tips I am sharing with you in this book, this tip is probably the most essential to living a thrifty life: think outside the box.

Thrifty people are known for seeing opportunities where others don't. My husband is very good at this. When we ripped out a giant, outdated furnace from the basement of our $10,000 home, he saw the two large, metal rings inside as lawn art for us and a fire pit for a friend.

I once took shorts that were too small for my son and made them into a skirt for his younger sister.

My husband took gym mats and made them into Roman Armor for our church play, and let me tell you, they looked nothing like cheap gym mats when he was done; they looked like real leather.

When the springs inside our couch broke, instead of running to the store for a new couch, my husband used bungee cords to replace the springs. When the bungee cords snapped, he cut a wooden board to sit on top of the springs and take our weight. These fixes added years of life to our couch.

I could list a dozen more ways my husband and I have saved our family money by thinking outside the box, but what I want most is for you to think this way.

If you have never really thought creatively, it can take awhile to switch gears. Here are four ways my husband and I activate our creative thinking:

Browse the Internet for Ideas

My favorite place for finding out-of-the-box thrifty solutions to our problems is *Pinterest*. I enter keywords relating to the problem I want to fix into the search area. For instance, when I need to give a gift but don't have money to go out and spend, I might enter the craft supplies I have on hand (such as "yarn" or "scrap fabric") and see what ideas pop up. Usually in a very short amount of time I will find something I can alter to fit my needs.

My husband, however, prefers an old fashioned *Google* search, which usually ends in him watching *YouTube* video after *YouTube* video.

Wander The Aisles

Another way my husband and I have saved a ton of money is by taking a few extra minutes to walk the entire aisle of the hardware store when we need to fix a problem in our home, instead of just going straight to the item we know will fix it. By doing this we have found alternative fixes that have saved us a significant amount of money.

This doesn't work just at the hardware store; it can be done at the craft store, the thrift store, and even the grocery store.

Engage In Disengaging Activities

Sometimes my best out-of-the-box thinking comes when I am able to disengage my brain and just let it wander. For me, this happens most often when I am out walking or running, but for others it might be while you wash the dishes or while you are taking a shower.

To take full advantage of my brainstorming activities, I will often write my "Oh, that is brilliant!" thought down in the notes section of my iPhone and then take a picture of it (because somehow my brilliant self often deletes notes by accident, so my photos have proved to be a great back-up filing system).

Head To Your Local Library

There is just something about digging into a pile of books pertaining to your problem that causes you to start seeing things in new ways.

My husband did this when he was working on our home. He wasn't the best at doing trim corners but really didn't want the expense of hiring the trim job out to someone, so he went to the library and picked up a pile of books on trim. He didn't find a solution for how to become better at corners inside the pages of the books (at least not one that made sense to him), but he did discover a beautiful, decorative way to hide his corner cuts that had a lower cost than hiring the job out.

Snail-Pacing Action Step

Next time you are faced with a need, don't pick up your wallet to run to the store and replace the item; instead wait a day or two and spend some time brainstorming solutions.

Thrifty People Are
Legacy-Builders

One of my desires for my children as they grow up and live their own lives is that they would be wise stewards of their time, talents, and money.

The first two aspects of stewardship are topics for a different book. For this book I am going to stick to how I am teaching my children to steward their money well.

To me, being a wise financial steward means using our talents to earn an income and stretching it as far as it can go.

I have done my best to teach that definition of financial stewardship to my children in the following ways.

1 Model It

From day one my kids have seen me shop yard sales, thrift stores, and clearance racks. They have also seen me use coupons, discounted gift cards, and gift cards earned through point programs (more on what point programs are in the chapter "Thrifty People Know You Need the Right Size Shovel").

2 Talk About It

Not only have my kids seen me doing thrifty practices, but they have also heard me talk about why I do them. From very early on I would say things like "Because I saved money by... we can afford to do...," keeping my script as simple as their level of understanding.

Now that they are much older, I help them think through their own purchases. "Could you save money on that video game by waiting a few months?" "Could you get a secondhand copy of that book?" "Do you want to rent the game overnight from *Redbox* first, just to make sure there is enough play value in it before buying it?" "We are going yard sale shopping this weekend, do you want to see if we find something similar then for less?"

I also want my children to understand that we trade our work hours for purchases, so from time to time I will say something like "Your father worked a full two hours to fill the gas tank in our vehicle for the week." These sorts of comments have made my children aware of their own work hour trades as I have heard them say "That video game would take a month of allowance to earn. I think I will look at the online reviews to make sure it has enough play value."

3 Take Them Along

I will admit that when my kids were little I left them home, if I could, when going to community yard sales or

thrift store one-day bag sales, just because it was easier
— and frankly, some days it was safer. It does not take
long for a child to disappear while you are busy going
through a pile of secondhand clothes.

Once they got older and I could trust them not to
run off when I turned my back, I began bringing one or
all of them to various thrifty events like yard sales or
thrift store one-day sales. I had them bring their own
spending money, so they could get a personal taste of
just how far money can go when you shop frugally.

4 Show Them Their Savings

The first time I brought my daughter along to a
community-wide rummage sale, I did something
afterwards that she still talks about today. When we
came home, I looked up on *Amazon* and other websites
everything that she had bought with her own money at
the rummage sale and showed her how much it would
have cost new, and then had her calculate her savings.
She saved about $70 that day, and that was an eye-
opening experience that had her thinking of all the
things she could buy used.

5 Make Them Set Goals And Work For Their Items

One of my sons saved up for his own computer. He
didn't just go into the store and buy one. He did some
research and realized he could build the computer he
wanted for less money. He watched *Youtube* videos for
months as he waited for his savings to add up. It made

my thrifty heart swoon to find him comparing prices in advance so that he would know the cheapest sources for buying the parts when the time came.

My daughter is the pennywise princess of our family. Before she turned twelve she had bought her own American Girl doll, a stereo, and an ipod! Let me tell you, her allowance is not that big; this thrifty mom only pays an average of $1 per chore.

How we pay them has changed over the years, as they have grown and needs have changed. One thing that remains the same, however, is that the pay is tied to a task, and it isn't much money. The pay is low because we feel that they should help out around the house not just for pay, but also because they are a part of the family. A family makes a mess together, so a family should clean the mess together.

However, they have been able to earn more by doing additional work for us that goes beyond housework, such as helping us do tasks at our rental homes. They have also earned money by reselling their own items that they no longer use.

6 Help Them Understand How To Prioritize Money

A few years back my daughter came to her father and I complaining that all of her friends saw all the latest movies at the movie theater as a family and we NEVER did. My husband and I first pointed out her error, as we do see one to three new-release movies a year, and not all of her friends see new-release movies all the time.

Secondly, we pointed out to her how much seeing a new-release movie costs a family of our size and then had her calculate what that cost would be over the course of a year if we saw one twice a month (about the frequency her friends' families were going to them).

Finally, we pointed out to her the things we do partake in as a family that her friends don't, and how our activities equal out in value to her friends' movie-going habits. This led to a talk about prioritizing money. We explained that we are all only given so much money to work with, and we each must choose what is the wisest way to spend it for our family; and that is going to differ from family to family due to values, talents and personalities.

7 Teaching Our Kids What The Bible Has To Say About Money

As Christians, my husband and I go one step further than the above six points and make sure that with every talk about money we also talk about what the Bible has to say about it.

There are over 3,000 verses in the Bible on the topic of money, so we never run out of verses to share with the kids. The ones that come up in our conversations the most, though, are those on being a wise steward and on giving.

My children know that the Bible says that we are to be wise stewards of what God entrusts to us, and that we firmly believe that being a wise steward lines up with being thrifty. They also know that being thrifty has allowed our family to give to others in ways we would not be able to otherwise.

Snail-Pacing Action Step

Take some time to reflect on what you are teaching your children about financial stewardship. Pick one action that you could take to improve in this area.

For instance, perhaps you need to ask your children to set a savings goal and then help them figure out how they can meet their goal.

Further Resources

For links to articles about how our family has set up simple chore systems for our children over the years, go to the resource page for this book at http://snailpacetranformations.com/thrifty-resources.

SECTION TWO:

Thrifty People Do

Thrifty People Do
PRACTICE CONTENTMENT

Being content is really hard, which is why I made the title of this chapter "Thrifty People Do Practice Contentment" instead of "Thrifty People Are Content."

"Contentment" to me is a verb; it is an action I do over and over each day. Every time I turn on *HGTV* while on vacation (we don't have cable at home — too thrifty for that!) I have to use every bit of my contentment training. There are people out there who spend more on their kitchens than my family did on our entire home including the remodel; and wow, those kitchens are amazing.

Learning to practice contentment is something that thrifty people know is vital to living the thrifty life successfully.

Being content saves money. Let's face it: we buy a lot of things we don't really need, just because we are discontented with what we already own.

Thrifty people have tools in their thrifty tool belt that help battle discontentment.

Thrifty people count their blessings

Thrifty people know that the best way to battle discontentment is to list their blessings on a regular basis.

The best way I have found to be content with what I have is to list my blessings daily. Every night before bed I write down in a simple journal a few lines full of things that happened that day that I am thankful for.

Thrifty people block out discontentment triggers

Another practice that helps is avoiding things that trigger discontentment. I have learned that there are certain *HGTV* programs I should not even watch because they automatically breed discontentment. I stay out of certain stores because they give me a good case of "I want, I should have, why don't I."

Thrifty people believe in the power of the small splurge

Sometimes you just get stuck in a bad "Why can't I have that?" attitude rut, and all it takes to get you out of it is a small thing. Perhaps a cup of your favorite coffee. Or a new album for your iPod. Or a trip through the dollar spot at *Target.* Or perhaps a new book.

Thrifty people know this, and so they have a small splurge category built into their budget. If the thrifty person is married, generally both the husband and wife have their own small splurge allotment that they can spend each month on little things that keep them happy and content. Or they can save it up and buy bigger items, if that is more their thing.

Thrifty people have visuals

Nothing helps stop discontent faster for a thrifty person than knowing they are not getting A because they are saving for B —and that they will make progress by staying on target.

You don't have to get all geeked out with pie charts if that isn't you. A simple picture that represents what you are saving for, posted on your fridge, is enough to trigger a move from discontentment to contentment.

Thrifty people hang out with other thrifty people

It is easier to live thrifty when your friends are thrifty. You might be using coupons on groceries so you can get out of debt, and I might be using them so I can take the family on vacation; but we both are using them to reach financial goals. Chances are that will bond us together and keep us accountable to staying on track.

Thrifty people give

Even when thrifty people are in the midst of pinching pennies to rid themselves of debt, they still give. Even if it is just a bag full of coupon-bought groceries dropped off at the local food bank or personal products donated at the nearest homeless shelter.

Thrifty people know that in giving we feel blessed, and when we feel blessed we are content.

Thrifty people take time to list priorities

Sure, your friend has a shiny new car, and you have a beaten-up clunker sitting in your driveway; but somehow it is easier to accept if you know the reasons behind having the clunker. Is keeping a clunker helping you or your spouse stay home with your little ones? Perhaps the clunker is helping you climb your way out of debt. Know your life priorities, and suddenly the sacrifices seem worth it.

Next time you badly want that item that another has, step back a second and think about your current priorities. If you set them right, they should be so much more valuable to you than breaking the budget to purchase that item you are envying.

Thrifty people keep a wish list

Sometimes when a wave of discontentment hits, an "I gotta have it now, and I don't care about the cost" mood can cloak our sanity; and the next thing we know we are facing a huge financial setback in reaching our money goals.

Thrifty people tackle this by putting the item on a wish list. I talk more about this in the next chapter.

Snail-Pacing Action Step

Over the next few weeks, pay attention to where you are when a wave of discontentment starts. Is it a place you could avoid or a show you could stop watching? Sure, you can't avoid going to your sister-in-law's grand home in the subdivision you cannot currently afford, but you can avoid the shopping mall or the home design magazine that fills you with "I want it."

For me, this action has made the biggest difference in my attitude of gratitude.

Further Resources

For a list of blog posts that I have written about this topic, visit the resource page for this book at http://snailpacetransformations.com/thrifty-resources/.

Thrifty People Do
KEEP A WISH LIST

In the pages of our thrifty family's financial binder you will find what our family calls "the wish list."

Most of the things on the list are not really wishes. Instead they are upcoming irregular expenses that we wish to fund. Things like vacations, household projects, and big purchases like furniture. Things that are fun but not necessary, so they are not included in our bare bones budget.

Beside each item we place the dollar figure of what we "wish" to spend and then fund that account to that level. We often don't spend the whole amount saved, due to finding a better deal than we thought; and when this happens we put the money left towards the next wish.

The wish list has also come in handy to curb spur-of-the-moment spending. If my husband or I want an item we see in the store, the item goes on the wish list. Sometimes before the item reaches top priority on the wish list, the person who put it there doesn't really want it anymore.

This practice makes us really think through each purchase and helps us not waste our money on items we don't really need. It also keeps us from feeling chained to a budget, because nothing is really off limits as long as we can save up the cash for it.

The wish list has paid off in other ways too. For instance, my husband really wanted a new couch. I agreed ours was getting very worn but didn't think it was a priority for our money right that second. Weeks later we saw a leather couch and chair for a great price at *Sam's.* We noted the price and moved the couch further up the wish list.

The next time we went to *Sam's,* the couch set was marked down by $200. My husband wanted to divert money from other "wishes" so as to take advantage of the sale, but I wasn't so sure yet. Another month went by and the couch set dropped in price again, making it ½ price. At that point my husband and I sat down with our wish list and diverted money that had been saved for other wishes towards paying for the couch instead. By waiting patiently, we paid less for our brand new couch set than most used ones similar to ours listed on *Craigslist.*

THE WISH LIST IS ALL ABOUT PATIENCE, COMPROMISE, AND OMMUNICATION.

You will note we took money from one wish to put it on another wish, essentially borrowing money from ourselves. We allow ourselves to do this for wish list items because they are wants, not needs, and therefore can be put off a few months more if need be.

Our family funds wish list accounts with money earned through my husband's overtime and my blog. Since we don't know just how much these earnings will be from month to month, we do not like depending on them to fill regular budget needs like food and shelter. We of course restock the emergency fund first, if need be, then move on to our wish list.

Some months, overtime and blog money are high and emergencies are low, and we can knock off one item on our wish list in a short amount of time. Other months, overtime and blog money are in short supply or emergency expenses have popped up; and so our wish list sits and waits.

If we really want an item on the wish list to be funded in a hurry, we will hold what we call a *Craigslist* blitz or a *Facebook* buy-and-sell group spree, selling items we no longer use to fund the wish.

What my thrifty family loves about the wish list is that it gives life to the "give each penny a purpose" way of budgeting. Before overtime money or blog money is even earned, we know exactly where it is going, and therefore we don't mismanage it on little, unmeaningful things like extra takeout pizza.

The wish list is all about patience, compromise, and communication. It is the most talked-about area of our finances in our home, because let's face it: projects, vacations, and major purchases are all more fun to talk about than food, the gas bill, and medical bills.

What To Do When You Stumble On Amazing Deals That Won't Last

You are in Target and you see they have sheet sets marked down 75% off, and you know yours are almost see-through. They were not on your wish list, but there are only two sets left, and you know if you don't grab them now they will soon be gone. What would a thrifty person do?

In our thrifty family, if the item is under $20 and truly something that will soon be a need (and to me sheets to cover the bed are a need), then as long as I know that I can "borrow" the money from another wish, I will grab them. I do have to be super disciplined to stick to only fast-approaching needs in these types of situations, since they do slow down other wish list goals. So that means I don't go sticking items like 90-percent off candlesticks and decorative pillows into my cart in addition to those marked-down sheets.

Snail-Pacing Action Step

Create your own family wish list. Come up with three to six things beyond basic bills that you would like to fund over the next twelve months.

After you have your list, discuss ways to make those things happen. Refer to the chapter "Thrifty People Know You Need the Right-Size Shovel" or "Thrifty People Do Sell To Buy" for ways to raise the money to fund items on your wish list.

Further Resources

For a list of ways we raise funds for our wish list, visit the resource page for this book found at http://snailpacetransformations.com/thrifty-resources/.

Thrifty People Do
USE WINDFALLS WISELY

If I were to pick one thing that has allowed us to become and stay 100% debt free — including the house — on a Registered Nurse's income, it wouldn't be our thrifty lifestyle. And it wouldn't be my husband's overtime income, his second job, or the income from my blog.

It wouldn't even be the money we received from several inheritances along the way, although obviously those did help. You see, we have received six inheritances from loved ones over the past 21 years of our marriage. Combined, they equal enough to buy one nice home in most North American real estate markets.

So what was the one thing that allowed us to become and stay 100% debt free? It wasn't the fact that we received the windfalls (inheritances) but rather how we used them. We took what most people would spend on one home and made it stretch to pay off student loan debt and vehicle debt, purchase and repair three homes with cash, and buy a few key things I needed to start my blog.

Our thrifty family put a lot of thought and prayer into how we spent every nickel of the several inheritances we received. We took our windfalls and harnessed their power to create maximum impact on our finances.

We did have a little bit of fun with the money, as well — but even the fun we had was done with much consideration. We thought about how much from each inheritance we wanted to devote for fun, and then we thought about what type of fun we wanted. We opted for memory-making trips, like a family trip to Disney World; and memory-making items, such as an RV to camp in.

THESE THINGS DIDN'T ADD TO OUR FINANCIAL PORTFOLIO BUT DID ADD DEPTH TO OUR FAMILY RELATIONSHIPS.

Only a small percentage of the inheritance money (windfalls) was spent on memory-making fun, though. The majority of it was spent in a way that would help us become better set up for a strong financial future.

With no debts to our name, my husband was able to give up a second job, where he worked 12-hour shifts both days every other weekend, and replace it with an on-call job, since we no longer needed those funds to make our bare-bones budget. Now if he gets extra work, it goes towards restocking our emergency fund or paying for items on our wish list.

Words cannot express how much more fun this makes extra work for my husband. He used to work a second job just to make sure we could eat and pay our debts; now he works a second job mostly so that we can enjoy extra things like a week of camping or have money for supplies to redo a room in our home.

The month-to-month income from one rental is basically what is keeping us out of auto debt, since what we pocket is about the same amount as we save each month in a savings account marked "auto replacement." In this way we can hopefully avoid vehicle debt for the rest of our lives.

We are currently still renovating the second rental; but when it is finished, the funds from it will help our children with their college costs.

The portion of the inheritance that we used to purchase the laptop I am typing this book on, a beginner's blogging conference ticket, and a DSLR camera has been creating a new income stream for us. This income stream continues to grow as the children need me less and less, and I can spend more and more hours growing the blog.

The blogging income stream is allowing us to replenish our emergency fund at a faster rate, and it is currently helping to pay for our eldest son to go to college through an inexpensive yet reputable online program.

We made all this happen with our windfalls because we made key thrifty choices. We live in a so-so neighborhood. It is safe, but not pretty; there are several homes in bad repair on our street.

The rental homes we bought were foreclosures that needed cosmetic work but are in good neighborhoods. My husband, being handy, did the majority of the work himself. I am the chief painter. I also used to do most of the grunt work that didn't require much skill, but since our children have grown they now do it for us and receive money in return.

Even the splurges we made were done in thrifty ways. For our trips, we rented places where we could eat in, and we drove instead of flying. We used coupons and applied discounts to our purchases and trips whenever we could.

By making these key thrifty choices, we were able to take money that we could have easily spent on just one property and make it go much, much further in meeting our financial needs and wants.

Snail-Pacing Action Step

Come up with your windfall plan before a windfall happens. That way you won't even think of your windfall as bonus money that you can just spend on this and that. Instead you will use it wisely, in a way that will pay back in dividends.

You might be thinking, "There is no way I will receive windfalls totaling what your family has received." Although that might be true, it is also true that small windfalls can add up over time; and when each is used wisely, the combined impact on your family's financial future can be huge.

Your windfall might be a tax return, a Christmas bonus check, or perhaps you find a treasure in your attic and discover it is worth a pretty penny.

Do not think of these windfalls as splurge money, as many seem to do, but see them as chances to get ahead financially; so that you have more wiggle room in your budget to splurge every day, not just when a windfall comes your way.

Think outside the box as to how you can best use your windfall to either create space in your budget or develop a new stream of steady income; then use a portion of that new income to save for a splurge!

Further Resources

To read our entire debt-free story from start to finish, visit the resource page for this book found on *Snail Pace Transformations* at http://snailpacetransformations. com/thrifty-resources/.

Thrifty People Do
MAKE NEW HABITS

You can succeed with each and every thrifty tip given in this book if you are willing to do one thing: form new habits.

Thrifty people have done this successfully, and that is why they appear to be living on less with ease.

Not every thrifty practice was easy for them at one time, but slowly each thrifty practice became a thrifty habit. And once something is a habit, it can be done with little thought or energy.

Thrifty people know that forming thrifty habits is never completely done. You are always forming new ones as you find new ways to save.

Right now I am trying to make it a habit to upload my receipts into my smartphone apps each and every time I grocery shop so that I can add to my savings on groceries.

I recently formed the habit of opening my *Shopkick* app whenever I enter *Meijer* or *Walmart* in my town, to claim walk-in points if they are available. I can then trade in those points for a gift card once I have enough.

The best ways I have discovered to make something a habit are to place reminders everywhere, make it hard to return to your default habit, chart your progress, and reward your small successes as well as your big.

Of course you have to decide what money-saving action you want to make a habit first.

Let's take my example of wanting to use my cashback apps for groceries each and every time I shop.

To make it happen, I could place a reminder on the fridge so that I see it as I am putting my new groceries away. There is really no way to return to a default habit here, since I didn't use apps at all before. I could chart my progress by placing a star on my calendar each time I use the app after grocery shopping, and I could celebrate my small success by spending the first cashout I receive on something just for me — like a Starbucks gift card for coffee.

When I have a plan, I do better at making sure it happens when I tell someone who will hold me accountable about it, such as my husband, who is — of course! — my partner in thriftiness.

Snail-Pacing Action Step

Take some time over the next few days to come up with one thrifty habit you could begin that would significantly change your family's budget. (I always like my first habit in a specific area to make a significant change, so I can see dramatic results to push me to make more habits in that area.)

Once you form that habit, form another (the second one can be smaller), and another and another. Soon you will see the power that compounding habits has on your family's finances.

Thrifty People Do
Dig Green

In this chapter I am referring to green as in green living, not green as in money — although thrifty people like that shade of green, too.

It is because thrifty people prefer to be good stewards of the money kind of green, in fact, that they also share a love of being environmentally green.

Right off the bat, I am going to agree with all the nay-sayers that are currently thinking in their heads, "but living green is expensive!"

Yes, some elements of living green are indeed expensive. Redoing your entire house with eco-friendly building supplies is going to add up fast.

However, other elements of the green movement are going to save you money.

The green movement pushes for environmentally safe cleaners

Commercially made green cleaners can be expensive; however, their homemade counterparts are dirt cheap.

A quick *Pinterest* search for homemade cleaners will give you hundreds of recipes for green cleaners that cost pennies to make and work just as well as commercially-made ones.

The green movement pushes for smaller homes

On the heels of the green movement is the tiny-house movement. Eco-friendly families want to decrease their environmental footprint as much as possible by living in a dwelling with the smallest square footage as they possibly can.

Now, I am not about to move my thrifty family of five into a 500-square-foot home, but I don't think our family needs to upgrade from our 2000-square-foot home, either.

I think we can all agree that smaller homes are less money to maintain and less money to heat and cool. Thrifty people think long and hard about just how many square feet they need in a home.

The green movement pushes for less consumerism

Less consumerism is always good for the wallet. The less you buy, the less money you spend.

You have already read the words "Do you really need it?" in this book several times, and that is because to me it is the ultimate thrifty question. It is a question that is also green.

When you walk away from a purchase, you walk away from the environmental impact of that purchase as well.

The green movement pushes for long-lasting items

It is green and thrifty to buy good quality items, as they will last longer and therefore reduce waste and the price of replacement. (I touch more on this in the chapter "Thrifty People Do Think About More Than Just Price.")

The green movement pushes for homegrown veggies

Lovers of green living are big fans of backyard organic gardens. Thrifty people love gardens, too!

A garden not only helps families eat locally-grown, pesticide-free, fresh produce; but it also saves families money on their grocery bills.

The green movement pushes for reusing & repurposing items

Green-living people want to see as few items as possible land in the garbage. Not only is this a green-living action, it is also a thrifty-living action. A thrifty person will reuse an item until it has no use left. This green practice doesn't just save the earth — it saves money.

The green movement pushes for more environmentally-sound sources of transportation

Green-living people are not fans of gas-guzzling vehicles, and neither are thrifty people.

Although a thrifty person probably isn't going to go to the expense of buying an electric car, they do consider gas mileage when picking out a vehicle; and they typically go for the smallest vehicle with the best gas mileage that still fits their family comfortably.

Thrifty people walk and bike to errands close by when they can; and depending on where they live, they may look into a form of public transportation to help meet their transportation needs. Thrifty people will also combine errands to save on gas and wear-and-tear on their vehicle.

I could go on and on with examples, but I think you are probably grasping the concept by now. Thrifty people pay attention to the green-living movement because often, but not all the time, it won't just save the earth, but it will also save money.

Snail-Pacing Action Step

Having just read all the ways that being green can be thrifty, pick the one thing on the list that you think will have the greatest impact on your budget and start applying it to your life.

Thrifty People Do
Make it Last Longer

From squeezing the last amount of toothpaste out of the tube to fixing the vacuum hose with duct tape, thrifty people make everything last as long as possible. By making things last longer, we reduce our need for more — because more always costs money.

There are five key ways a thrifty person can make something last longer. They can use less, take good care of it, repair it, get one more use out of it, and repurpose it.

Use Less

If you came into our home, here is a way you would find us using less. You would find a foaming hand soap container not just beside the bathroom sink, but near the kitchen sink where it is filled with dish soap, and in the shower where it is filled with body wash. When the bottles are empty, we fill them with 1/3 soap and 2/3 water and then let the foaming pump do its work of making our soap go a long way.

Take good care of It

One year into blogging I made two big investments: a *Mac* laptop and a *Canon* DSLR camera. I am super picky about where I will put my laptop and camera down and what I will have near them. I avoid having liquids on the same surface that either one sits on. I put them in my room when not in use so that my boys can't accidentally knock them over when they are roughhousing.

Repair it

Around our thrifty home we specialize in two types of repairs: the "good-enough repair" and the "traditional repair."

The good-enough repair

A great example of the good-enough repair in our home is the vegetable crisper in our fridge that is held together with packing tape (I thought it looked less ugly than duct tape).

It doesn't fully fix the problem — the drawer is still broken — but a new drawer was going to be $50, and the packing tape was something I already owned. It made the drawer workable again, so it is "good enough."

The traditional repair

When our dryer started getting louder and louder with each load, we put up with the noise for awhile, until it started taking much longer than normal to dry our clothes. At that point we googled how to repair it. My husband felt the job was beyond his DIY capabilities, so we hired a repairman to come to our home and fix the dryer. In the end it cost us less than buying a secondhand dryer off *Craigslist* and certainty much less than a new one.

Get one more use out of it

Rolling up the end of the toothpaste tube is a classic example of this one. As is the well-known trick of taking the lid off the shampoo and putting a bit of water into the bottle, swishing it around, and then dumping it on top of your head for just one more shampooing.

These are not the only ways to get more use out of things. Next time you think a product is empty, take a minute to think creatively if there isn't some way you could squeeze just a bit more out of it.

Repurpose it

When an item is beyond repair or simply no longer needed for its intended purpose (e.g., outgrown clothing), it still might be useful — just not in the way it was intended to be.

This is when thrifty people head to *Pinterest* to look for ideas on how they could transform those outgrown jeans into gifts to give, or how to use all those free t-shirts they keep getting at events to make a cool t-shirt rug like the one they saw in their neighbor's home.

SNAIL-PACING ACTION STEP

Next time you think that you should replace an item, ask yourself if you can't use one of the five key thrifty principles for making it last longer.

FURTHER RESOURCES

For a list of different ways our family uses things to the last drop, visit the resource page for this book found at http://snailpacetransformations.com/thrifty-resources/.

Thrifty People Do
EVALUATE NEED VERSUS WANT

Thrifty people know that very few things in this world are actually needs. Thrifty people's budgets reflect this knowledge.

Using our thrifty family as an example, I want to share how we decide what makes the budget and what doesn't by evaluating need versus want.

When I created our family's budget for the first time years ago, I started with listing my husband's average take-home pay after tithe. I know that it is unusual to budget in an "after-tithe" way, but as Christians my husband and I find it easier to simply think of our tithe as already given before it even hits our bank account. After all, it was never ours to begin with — it is God's.

I then subtracted needs such as food, shelter costs, medications, and a very basic clothing allowance.

Next I added in what I would call the "most mislabeled want in North America"— vehicles and the expenses that come with them. Yes, a vehicle is a want. It is possible, although very inconvenient, to live without one; and yet many of us, including my own family, refuse to live without at least two.

After vehicle costs came our student loan payments. On our budget we always wrote down just the minimum payment, but rarely did we pay just the minimum payment (more on that in a second).

Finally my husband and I started discussing which wants were most important to us. For example, we wanted cell phones. We discussed just how much we wanted to spend on those cell phones. Did we want the newest and greatest and the price tag that came with them? Could we be okay with older models using pay-as-you-go companies and apply the difference we saved to more wants that we wanted?

On and on went the "want" discussions. Did we need cable? Or could we live with local channels only brought in with rabbit ears (this was the day before digital TV's and *Netflix*)?

In the end our budget became a list of needs and wants. Our list of needs is pretty much like every other family (with the exception, I suppose, of how many medications your family might need compared to mine). Our list of wants reflects our personalities, our passions, and our values.

A FURTHER WORD ON DEBT REPAYMENT

Above I stated that during the years we were in debt, we rarely just paid the minimum on our student loan.

How did we do that? While we had our student loans, we kept our "wants" extremely small . We constantly asked ourselves "Do we really need this?" before we made even the smallest of purchases so that we could always throw more than the minimum payment on the smallest loan left to pay. Trust me, we were brutal with ourselves when it came to deciding what was a "want" and what was a "need".

For instance, our family endured several summers of all five of us sleeping in one room because we only had one single one-room air conditioning unit, and we considered purchasing another one to be a luxury — something that could be put off until all debts were paid.

We drove a $250 car in which you had to keep your feet simultaneously on both the gas and the brake at stop lights; otherwise, it would stall out.

Once the smallest loan was paid, we moved on to the next smallest, adding the amount of the previous payment onto the next, which is the classic debt snowball.

During this time we also worked like crazy to increase the size of our debt payment shovel. My husband sometimes worked 12 days in a row, and I managed a licensed family daycare so that we could generate more income to get rid of our debts faster.

We paid off a significant amount of what we owed in just a few short years this way. Then when the inheritance money came along, it paid off the last of the student loan debt, our vehicle loans, and the mortgage, making us 100% debt free.

Snail-Pacing Action Step

I challenge you to go through every line of your budget this week and label each item either a need or a want. Create a budget that puts needs first; then start adding the wants back in, and be brutally honest about just how much you really want in order to feel content. Remember: each want you say "yes" to costs you being able to say "yes" to another.

For others, once you make your bare-bones, needs-only budget, you might not have all that much room to add in many wants. You might get to add in the car and the pay-as-you-go cell phone, your debts, and then have no room left in your budget.

The solution to your financial problems, if you find your family is in that situation, is to increase your income. You may want to skip on over to the chapter "Thrifty People Know You Need The Right-Size Shovel" to see if you can't start increasing your income and thus the room in your budget for wants.

Thrifty People Do
Shop Their Homes First

Many generations ago, buying something new was a big deal. It took a lot of effort. You had to hitch up the wagon, load up the family, and make the long wagon ride to town. When you got there, the local shops might not even have what you wanted, and instead you would have to look it up in a catalog and order it.

Forget about one-day shipping! You had to wait months, sometimes, to get your packages.

Although I love the convenience of the modern world I live in, I think it comes with a few major drawbacks — one of them being that we no longer have to wait to purchase anything.

Not only does this lead to spontaneous purchases that quickly become clutter in our homes, it also has dulled our ability to look at things we already own, to see if they can meet our new needs.

Just the other day I put this thrifty lifestyle action into practice when I needed a stitch marker to help me with my knitting project. Instead of going to the store and getting one, I simply used a bead I already owned.

Another time I thought I needed shorts, but when I shopped my closet I realized I had several nice skirts that were getting totally neglected — so I just wore those that summer instead.

This Christmas I thought I needed Christmas snow for a light display, but then I remembered I had picked up some spider webbing on clearance after Halloween for another thrifty project my daughter was working on, and she had plenty to spare. It turns out spider webbing is essentially the same as Christmas snow if you don't take the time to stretch it all out.

Now that I run a blog in addition to homeschooling and keeping our home in order, I am using this thrifty principle more and more, as I am more aware of just how much time it takes to shop.

There is the driving to and from the store, the picking out, the checking out, and the driving home.

Even online shopping takes time. I don't know about you, but more often than not, online shopping takes more time than brick-and-mortar shopping, simply due to the large selection and all of the handy reviews that suck me in. Then there is the time spent waiting for the item to arrive and all the hassle of returning it should it not be what you wanted (even though you read all 30 reviews and were certain it was).

All this to say that I think the pioneers were onto something: save time and money and shop your home first before heading to shop either the brick-and-mortar way or the online way.

Snail-Pacing Action Step

This week, pick one item on your "to buy" list and see if you can't just shop your own home instead.

Thrifty People Do
Love Free Items

It shouldn't be any surprise to you that thrifty people love free items. There is not a thriftier way to save money than to not spend a dime.

Please note, though, that there is a difference between finding and enjoying free items vs. expecting or even demanding free items. Thrifty people do not expect to get anything for free; but we are extremely thankful when we do find a free item, and we do our best to use it well and share it with others.

Finding free items is not as difficult nowadays with all the great blogs out there sharing deals — as well as all the social media sites that make sharing free deals so simple.

Thrifty online sources for finding free items

These sites offer both low-cost deals and free deals. You can find the links to all of these sites on the resource page for this book found at http://snailpacetransformations.com/thrifty-resources/.

Money Saving Mom: A great site for finding free samples, Redbox movie rental codes, and much more.

Freebies4mom: Continually updated list of free samples available online.

Free Homeschool Deals: If you homeschool on a shoestring budget, this site is a must.

Spirit-Filled Kindle*:* I love reading both Christian fiction and nonfiction, and *Spirit-Filled Kindle* keeps my *Kindle* filled with great free titles.

Smart Apps For Kids: Most of the free apps listed on Fridays on *Smart Apps For Kids* are for younger children, but if your children are older it is still worth following. I got our entire high school Spanish curriculum free of charge through *Smart Apps For Kids*.

Free Cycle: I haven't had any personal experience with *Free Cycle*, as it isn't very active in our area, but I have seen other bloggers pick up incredible finds like free children's bikes through *Free Cycle*. It is definitely worth looking into to see if it is active in your area.

Other Places To Find Free Items

Your local paper: Your local paper (or the paper's website) is a great place to find out about free events in your area that could make for great free family entertainment.

Your library: A library card is found in way more wallets of thrifty people than a credit card. Thrifty people know that their local libraries are a treasure trove of free resources.

Our library has free storytimes, free art lessons, free knitting lessons, and of course free books and DVD's to borrow. Summertime reading programs provide a huge bounty of free rewards — from coupons for free food at local restaurants to free tickets to the local water park.

Facebook: Thrifty people follow their favorite companies on *Facebook* and click the "get notifications" area for those companies that share free offers and samples on a regular basis.

Companies are not the only source of free items on *Facebook* though. Thrifty people know that when they have a need it never hurts to ask their Facebook friends to help fulfill it, because they know they themselves would help another if asked.

My one friend hit the free item gold mine when she simply asked if her flower-gardening *Facebook* friends had plants they were thinning out in spring that she could take for her garden. She got enough free plants to fill a huge garden bed.

App of the Day: This app shares free apps on a daily basis. My children have gotten great games through it.

Company loyalty programs: The key to enjoying free items with loyalty programs the thrifty way is to make sure they are not causing you to buy more just so you can get the free item.

However, if it is a place you would go to even if they didn't offer you free things, then go for it! Sign up and enjoy free benefits now and again.

I love loyalty programs so much that I have devoted an entire chapter to them in the "Thrifty People Know" section of this book.

Birthday clubs: Birthday clubs differ from loyalty clubs in that they reward you typically just once a year on your birthday. The majority of birthday clubs are offered by restaurants, but other stores and companies do offer them.

I have included the link to the list of birthday clubs I enjoy in the Midwest in the resources section of this book, found at http://snailpacetransformations.com/thrifty-resources.

By no means is my list an exhaustive list of all the birthday freebies out there. A simple search via *Google* or *Pinterest* is going to bring up more birthday clubs for restaurants and stores that might be in your area but are not in mine.

Ask Personally: My husband once saw a brick building being demolished and asked one of the demolition crew what they were doing with the bricks. The worker asked, "Do you want some?" My husband said, "Sure." The worker then said, "Drive your truck over here and you can fill up with as many as you want for free." Those bricks made amazing borders around our flower beds. FREE is so wonderful.

Now, be aware that in order for "the thrifty ask" to work, both sides have to have a thrifty win. In the above scenario my husband was willing to bet that he would be told the bricks were free, because his hauling them away would save the company trash removal costs — and he was right. He put in several hours of work for his free pavers, but it was worth it for us, so both sides got a thrifty win.

Snail-Pacing Action Step

Look over the list above one more time, but this time pick out the source of free items that you think is going to have the biggest impact on your family's budget. Make it a habit and then pick another.

Thrifty People Do
BORROW OR RENT

Thrifty people know that sometimes the most economical way to acquire something is to first try it out and see if it is really something they truly want or need.

For instance, my boys love purchasing video games when they first come out. Even though it would be way more thrifty for them to wait to buy them, since the price drops as a game becomes older, I remember being a teenager and wanting the latest and greatest — so I have them rent it first.

The reason I have them rent it first is because I want them to make sure that the game truly does have as much play value as they think it will have. *Redbox* offers games at just over $2 for an overnight rental; that is plenty of time for my boys to test it and figure out if the game really is as good as the commercials say it is.

Many times renting the game makes them realize that it just isn't all that great. Other times, though, they discover that they really want it, and then I help them find ways to save as much money as they can on it; but at least I know the game will be played and enjoyed.

Being thrifty isn't about doing without; it is about making sure that you are wise with the money you have and making it work for you in a way that brings you joy. Borrowing or renting before you buy a non-need item is a great way to do just that.

Another reason to rent or borrow is for items you really won't use much. For instance, when we were renovating our current home, our previous home, and our rental, we rented certain tools instead of buying them. One home had wallpaper that just would not budge, so we rented a wallpaper steamer instead of buying it — because how often do you steam wallpaper? Another time we rented a jackhammer to tear apart a large concrete slab.

Before you buy a large item, think to yourself, "How many times will I use this?" If the answer is not many, see if you can borrow it or rent it.

Of course there is a third option for items you don't use much: purchase it used, use it, and then sell it right away for the same or more than you bought it for. We did this with a moving van.

Yes, a moving van. I thought my husband was crazy when he came home with a 20-year-old cube van and told me we were going to use it for the nearly 3,000 mile move from British Columbia, Canada to Indiana, USA. However, when he sold the truck just a few weeks after settling into our new home for the same amount he paid for it, essentially making our moving costs just gas, hotel, and food, he became a genius in my eyes.

Snail-Pacing Action Step

Next time you are considering a large purchase, think about borrowing or renting it first for a trial run. You might just discover you don't want it at all once you try it out. Also, weigh the option of renting or borrowing items that you won't use often.

Thrifty People Do
SELL TO BUY

There have been times in our marriage when it seemed like the best source we had to fund items on our wish list was the no-longer-needed possessions we had lying around the house.

Clothing would be an excellent example. When my children were little, it seemed like they changed sizes at least once a season, if not more often. By selling the clothes they grew out of, I could then afford to buy them clothes in their new size.

Another great example is toys. By selling the toys my kids were no longer playing with, I could afford to buy them a new toy for their birthday or as a Christmas gift. This was of course when they were toddlers or younger. When they got older, they got to decide which toys went in the yard sale; and they received the money from the sale of their toys.

Other times I already had gifts and clothing taken care of, but we wanted money to pay for an event the kids wanted to attend or for a camping vacation.

I want to give one word of caution about reselling: don't let piles build up around your home waiting for a window of time to sell them. Either make selling them a priority or give them to charity; a cluttered home is too high a price to pay for the amount of money you might make when you get around to reselling.

In past years I gave myself deadlines to avoid this, such as, "If I don't sell what is in this box by the end of the month, it goes to charity." I then created blocks of time each week that I devoted to reselling the items.

Now that we have a bit more wiggle room in our budget than we did when we were first married, I set a price limit on reselling items. If I can't resell it for at least $25, in the donation box it goes.

If you have difficulty letting go of items you know could be worth something, look for a thrift store that supports a cause you like. Our family gives our stuff to a locally-owned thrift store that provides hot lunches to the needy as well as clothing and food to take home.

Reselling takes time, and time is also money; make sure you are not selling things that are not going to pay you the hourly wage your time is worth. For instance, I know it is going to take me at least 15 minutes to list one single item on a *Facebook* buy-and-sell group. Then there is my time answering questions, time arranging an exchange of money for the item, time driving to the exchange point, doing the exchange, and driving home. Altogether that is a minimum of 2 hours. If I stick to my $25 minimum, that is $12.50 an hour for my effort, and that is worth it to me. Your personal worth level might be lower or higher depending on your financial need.

A few places to resell your items

I have written extensively on my blog about different ways to resell your items, and I have placed the links to those articles in the resource page for this book that you can find at http://snailpacetransformations.com/ thrifty-resources, but for now I want to share briefly all the different avenues you can use to resell your items.

Yard sale: Yard sales are still my favorite ways to raise a huge amount of money by reselling products in a hurry. I have made as much as $650 in one day by hosting a yard sale. The key is to prepare well and work your sale like it is a showroom all day long.

Consignment stores: Consignment stores are for more than just clothing. You can usually sell toys and baby items — there are also sporting goods consignment shops as well. The number one tip I would give for successful consignment shop selling is to know the store's sale policies inside and out.

Consignment sales: A consignment sale differs from a consignment store in that it doesn't have a permanent storefront but sets up for a short duration of time, usually one to three days. You do need to know the rules of the sale well for a successful consignment sale experience, but even more important is knowing what prices to charge for your items. Attending a sale in your area before selling at one helps in setting realistic prices.

Facebook buy-and-sell groups: Using *Facebook* groups to sell your items is so simple. Snap a picture, upload, write the description, and bam! Your item is for sale. Make sure to follow several local groups if you can, and read the feed in the group for awhile before you jump in. I found that this helped me decide which group seemed to be most active. It also helped me weed out a group where the sales seemed a bit shady.

Note to readers: At the time of this writing, *Facebook* has just recently launched their *Facebook Marketplace* area. I have yet to list anything on it, but it seems to me that this feature will quickly replace *Facebook* buy and-sell groups.

Craigslist: You can't beat the reach of *Craigslist*. I have had people come from hours away to pick up large items from me. You can sell smaller items together in one single lot, such as a box full of yarn for one set price; but I prefer *Craigslist* for big ticket items such as campers, cars, large appliances, and large furniture items.

eBay: *eBay's* customer base is larger than any other selling platform I know of. You can sell your items not just to those who live locally but to those who live across the world from you. There are, however, a lot of fees involved; and out of all the selling platforms, it has the biggest learning curve. There is a lot more to successfully selling on *eBay* than just snapping a picture and giving it a price. Still, if you are willing to learn a few things about selling on *eBay,* the profit margins can be very high, even with the fees *eBay* charges you.

Personal Facebook Page: Before there were *Facebook* buy-and-sell groups, I would make an album on my personal *Facebook* page that was labeled "virtual yard sale" and post pictures of items for sale. I had great success with it and still often list items this way.

Metal Recyclers: People often forget just how much money you can earn from broken metal items when you take them to a metal recycler. We once loaded up a pickup truck's worth of metal out of our home and made well over $100.

Secondhand Curriculum Sales: If you homeschool, do some research and see if there are any secondhand curriculum sales in your area. Typically these are held in late spring. I attend one in a neighboring city, and the time and effort expended to gather and price all the school materials we are no longer using is paid back in good financial returns the day of the sale.

Throw it on the front lawn: This isn't going to work in all neighborhoods, but at one place we lived I sold big items simply by hauling them out close to the road on a nice day and placing a "for sale" sign on them.

These next two options will result in store credit, but I think they are still worth mentioning since *Amazon* sells almost anything you could need or want. Plus, if you are selling video games, chances are that means you have a video game lover who would appreciate a gift card with which to purchase more video games.

Amazon Trade-In Program: The *Amazon Trade-In Program* works really well for books, video games, and certain small electronic devices (smartphones and such). I have used it twice for books, and it was so simple and quick. You get paid in *Amazon* gift card codes.

Gamestop: My video-loving boys have taken advantage of the *Gamestop* trade-in program on two occasions, and both times they were happy with the results.

These last three ideas I have not personally tried yet, but I thought I would mention them so that you could research them further and see if they might work for you.

Instagram: I simply entered "how to hold a yard sale on *Instagram*" into *Google*, and a list of very helpful articles popped up on how to do it effectively. The number one tip I saw was to set up a separate account just for your reselling so that you don't spam friends and family wanting to see pictures of your cute baby and not your old furniture. For more great tips, I suggest you do just what I did and enter "how to hold a yard sale on Instagram" into your search engine and spend some time reading the articles that pop up.

Pawn Shops: Again, do an internet search to find out how to successfully sell your items to a pawn shop. I tried "how to sell to pawn shops" and many great articles were listed, full of great advice to help you with your pawn shop sales.

Gold Stores: Do not sell family heirlooms that you will regret later. With that important guideline mentioned, gold catches a good price for resale. Again, the key is to do your research. Know what gold should resell for and which stores have a great reputation.

5 TIPS TO HELP YOU GET TOP DOLLAR FOR YOUR ITEMS

Preparation is everything

To get the most money possible for your items, it is very important that you take the time to prepare them.

You also need to gather the information needed to describe the item and price it well.

1. Clean your items well

The cleaner the item, the quicker it sells — and for more money, too.

Plastic toys: Buy a soft scrub cleaner or make your own and wash the whole toy down with it. For the really big toys like the plastic slides, take them outdoors to do this and then let it dry in the sun. If you still have some marks left, try a magic eraser.

Wooden furniture: Give it a good wash with Murphy's oil soap. Also take the time to tighten up legs and drawer pulls.

Clothing: Make sure your clothing is freshly washed and then folded so that it has the least amount of wrinkles. Hanging your clothes for sale is always best, but I know it is not always possible. If clothes have even a small stain or rip, don't mix them in with the clothes that don't — it turns off buyers. If you truly feel they still have value, put them all together in one area, let your customers know their flaws, and price accordingly.

2. Know your item's true worth

An overpriced item won't sell, and an underpriced item won't sell, either. I know the second one is hard to believe, but trust me. If I price an item too low, no one bites — this happens especially when I sell online. It could be because they think something is wrong with it.

If you don't have a clue what your item is worth, spend some time researching what the item goes for in your intended market. By this I mean that if you plan to hold a yard sale, spend a Saturday beforehand visiting other yard sales in your area, noting how much items similar to what you have to sell are priced. If you plan to sell your fridge on *Craigslist*, look at other listings of similar fridges first and see what they are selling for.

Remember that selling secondhand items means that you won't always get the price you're asking for. People love to haggle in the secondhand arena, and you will be expected to be willing to drop your price some. In other words, price your item with wiggle room for bargaining.

3. Showcase Your Item

How to showcase your item well depends on how you are selling it.

Yard Sale: Put like items together. Make sure your tables are neat and tidy and items are priced clearly. For larger items, put them out front to draw in customers. Make sure furniture is sitting on a level surface so that it doesn't appear wobbly when it really isn't.

Facebook buy-and-sell groups: You usually only get one picture for these types of groups, so make sure it is a good one, taken in great light and showing the best side of the item. You can also make a collage on Picmonkey, an online photo editing program, of all the sides of the item and then post that collage.

Craigslist: Craigslist allows you to display several photos. Make sure you use them to show the best parts of your item. I always like to be honest, too; so I not only list the flaws of my item, but I also include a picture of the biggest one (like a dent in the side of the washing machine).

eBay: Make sure the picture that will show up in the listing area is a great one — good lighting, close up, no background distractions.

4. Be knowledgeable about the item

I like to know a lot about the items I am selling. How old? How big? Its features. The pluses. The drawbacks.

If I am listing an item online, I always take the measurements of it and list them, as well as all of the above. This saves me a lot of time, as I have fewer email questions to answer.

Knowing these things really does help make the sale. Not many people want to buy an item that contains no details and for which they only get an "I don't know" for an answer.

5. Know the best platform to sell

Certain items sell better on different platforms than others. In general you can sell almost anything at a yard sale, but just because something didn't sell at a yard sale doesn't mean it won't sell at all. Your ideal customer may not have been out shopping that day.

Facebook buy-and-sell groups are also great places to sell just about everything (although to help keep time costs down I would group smaller, similar items into one large lot and sell them as a "one buyer gets all" deal).

A simple list of the best places to sell particular items (other than a yard sale or Facebook group)

- ***Clothing:*** Consignment stores & consignment sales

- ***Toys:*** eBay or consignment stores.

- ***Large items like appliances & furniture:*** Craigslist

- ***Books & Video Games:*** Try the *Amazon Trade-in* program for both or Gamestop just for video games.

Warning!

Reselling items can become addicting. Should this happen to you, rather than starting to sell things that others in the house might be upset about — like the TV and the couch — you might want to consider buying under-priced items and reselling them for profit.

This is a great way of creating a flexible stream of income. It is one that I pursued off and on for several years to help pay for swimming lessons, Christmas gifts, and more.

There are of course taxes that apply if you should earn a profit that exceeds the legal non-taxable limit, so make sure to keep good records and consult tax laws so you know how to follow them correctly.

Snail-Pacing Action Step

Pick one item in your house this week that you no longer need and try listing it in a *Facebook* buy-and-sell group. Once you are past that first sale anxiety, I think you will be amazed just how simple it was to sell the item and will start listing more.

Further Resources

For a link to all my articles on how to resell your items for top dollar, visit the resource page for this book at http://snailpacetransformations.com/thrifty-resources/. When you get there, you will also want to sign up for my weekly newsletter so that you can receive the "Thrifty & Thriving Printable Pack" that contains a checklist for reselling your items.

Thrifty People Do
THINK ABOUT MORE THAN JUST PRICE

Thrifty people know that when you consider a purchase you need to look beyond comparing price tags — you need to think of operating costs and more.

For instance, thrifty people know that when they are out shopping for a vehicle they need to research gas mileage, cost of repairs, and frequency of problems for the vehicle models they are interested in. In the end the car with the cheapest sticker price might not be the least expensive option; instead it may be the one that costs just a bit more due to its better gas mileage and reputation for not needing frequent repairs.

A thrifty person also knows that the cost of vacation is higher than the all-inclusive price tag found on the discounted travel website. The dog is going to need a sitter. The car is going to have to sit at the airport. There is a chance you might have to make up for income lost while you were off work. All of these things need to be included in your full vacation price.

This goes for things you are considering not buying, too. For instance, say you are thinking about doing away with your home internet. You think it is a doable sacrifice to make more room in the budget for things of higher priority.

Is that really a thrifty decision that will save you money, or will you end up spending more money on fancy coffee so you can sit around and use the coffee shop's internet? Will you end up spending more money on entertainment because you can no longer stream free TV and movies? Will your data usage on your smartphones go up — costing you overage fees — because you just can't stop checking *Facebook* one more time before bed?

Obviously you can come up with a thrifty solution to all I listed above — go to the library where they don't sell fancy coffee to use free internet, borrow some DVD's while you are there, practice self-discipline to stay within data limits — and providing you are willing to do them, then cutting internet is a wise choice.

Thinking through all the costs of an expense takes time. This is why thrifty people are not known for being impulsive. Instead they like to slowly consider the true cost of each and every purchase. The larger the price tag of the purchase, the longer the thrifty person usually takes to consider the true cost of the item.

SNAIL-PACING ACTION STEP

Next time you are facing a large purchase decision, take the time to think through all the costs associated with the purchase, beyond just the sticker price.

Sit down with a pad of paper and a pen and list what the purchase is truly going to cost you. Does it need a constant stream of ink, batteries, fuel, etc., to keep it going? What is the cost of that? Will it need repairs? Will it mean you need to pay storage fees to store it away from your premises in the off season (like a boat or RV)?

If you are purchasing an event like a vacation, think about all the extra expenses. Will you receive less income due to taking time off? Do you need to pay for parking? Do you need to get a house sitter? A dog sitter? What is the cost of fuel there and back? How much do you have to budget for food? Entertainment? Souvenirs? Accommodations?

Once you go ahead and purchase the item or event, take time to keep track of the true expense of the item to see if perhaps there is some cost that you forgot to consider or under- or overestimated so that you can make an even better buying decision next time.

Thrifty People Do
SOMETIMES PAY MORE

I think one of the biggest misconceptions about thrifty people is that we will always purchase the least expensive option.

That simply isn't true. There are several reasons why thrifty people are willing to purchase a higher-priced item or service, even though a similar, lower-priced item is available.

THRIFTY PEOPLE PAY MORE FOR QUALITY

I have made the mistake of falling for the "It's cheaper so I will save money buying it!" trap way too often. I am far from perfect in this key thrifty life practice.

The last time I did this it was buying the dollar store ice cube trays which broke in half after a week of repeated use. I then did some research on *Amazon* and invested in a set of name-brand ice cube trays that were significantly more than a dollar, but years later they are still going strong.

Sure, $1 wasn't a lot to waste to see if I could save money, but there have been more expensive mistakes than the ice cube trays. Over the years, as I have had to throw away broken, cheap item after broken, cheap item, I have learned to look not just at price but to also consider quality.

How a thrifty person considers quality

Compare the cheaper item to the more expensive. Does one item feel like it is made better? Check online for reviews before purchasing. Is there one brand of the item you are looking at that is said to hold up to repeated use better?

Also consider how many times you are going to use the item. If the usage is going to be daily, then the high quality and perhaps more expensive item is probably the way to go. If you are just going to use the item once in a blue moon, you might be able to get away with buying the less expensive option, even if it isn't as well-made.

One last thing to remember when buying higher quality is that just because you are buying the more expensive item doesn't mean you can't apply other thrifty practices to drive the price down as low as it can go. There are several thrifty practices in this book that can help you do so.

THRIFTY PEOPLE PAY MORE FOR GOOD CUSTOMER SERVICE

When our children reach adult size, we buy them a brand new bike from a locally-owned bike store. We do this because we know our children will own their adult bikes a long time, and if we have any problems with the bikes whatsoever, the owner of the shop will gladly fix them for us — often the same day, and for a very small fee.

We also buy our automobile tires from a local tire store. It is a chain store — but a smaller one. We love it because anytime our tires get a flat (which is crazy often), the store fixes it for us for free. They have also helped me get the tire pressure light on my dashboard to finally turn off.

It is true that both the bikes and the tires cost us more than what those found at big-box stores would cost us, but the customer service we have received has been worth every extra penny we spent and more. It has saved us both time and money.

Bad customer service experiences have caused my family to simply turn our backs on certain brands and stores, even though they offered lower prices. Our thrifty family has learned the hard way that if you are buying an item that will need repairs or regular maintenance, it is thriftier in the long run to pick the good customer service over the low price tag.

THRIFTY PEOPLE WITH THE MEANS SUPPORT SMALL BUSINESSES

Not every thrifty family is in the financial position to do this, but often when a thrifty family becomes blessed with a little more wiggle room in their budget, they like to pass the blessing on to small business.

It might be buying handmade items to use as gifts from a mom wanting to create enough monthly income to stay home with her children, instead of making those gifts ourselves.

It could be simply paying a bit more to buy regular, everyday items at a small, mom-and-pop shop instead of the big-box store down the street, because of the warm smile and hug we get each time we enter the smaller store.

It could mean buying eggs and vegetables from a local farmer at higher prices than the grocery store, because we know they will be healthier for our family; and we now have more wiggle room in our budget to pursue our healthy eating goals at a larger level.

Snail-Pacing Action Step

Next time you find yourself picking up the cheapest item, take a second to think about how long that item will last compared to the higher-priced item sitting on the shelf right beside it. Carefully consider if the higher-priced item just might be worth the extra money you spend on it.

Thrifty People Do
Not Buy it All at One Store

Thrifty people might shop at a one-stop store, but that won't be their only stop. Why? Because thrifty people know that there is no one store offering the lowest prices on everything — despite their claims.

My husband cringes when he hears that people not only bought their paint at the hardware store but also their paint supplies. You see, my husband buys our paint supplies at *Big Lots* because they are half the price there.

My son loves name-brand athletic shorts, but I don't buy them at the clothing store. Nope. I buy them at *Sam's Club* and save at least $5 per pair.

I also don't go to just one store when I go out grocery shopping. I hit three to four stores for our weekly grocery trip (although sometimes I stop at each one on different days if I am close to one that day for another errand I have to run).

In order to save the most money, people have to get out of the "pick it all up at one store" mentality.

Start paying attention to which store offers the lowest prices on certain items. Keep track of the prices of the items you buy again and again in a simple notebook for a while, until you know which store offers them for the least amount of money.

This thrifty principle doesn't just apply to brick-and-mortar retail shops but to other types of shopping environments, too.

Online versus in-store

Here is a thrifty secret that I don't really understand: I have found that the online prices for certain items at some big-box stores are better than their in-store prices, and often you can take advantage of free shipping or free ship-to-store options.

Our family has used this thrifty tip to save money on computer monitors and TVs.

Online versus online

A thrifty person compares prices from website to website just like they do from brick-and-mortar store to brick-and-mortar store.

I do this for my running shoes and often save as much as $20 per pair for just 5 minutes hopping from site to site to compare prices. That works out to an hourly wage of $240!

Secondhand buying options

Seasoned thrifty families know which secondhand stores and online platforms are the least expensive for certain items.

For instance, yard sales tend to beat the prices of all other secondhand buying options hands down, with *Facebook* buy-and-sell groups coming in at a close second.

From there I would say it goes from thrift stores to *Craigslist*, consignment stores, and then finally *eBay*. But again, it all depends on what you are searching for.

In time, if you stick to the thrifty lifestyle, you will also get to the point where you know which community-wide yard sales offer better prices, which thrift stores price things the lowest, and what not to buy at consignment stores; because you are now better armed with thrifty practices that can help you buy some things new at prices better than the consignment store.

Snail-Pacing Action Step

Pick four items this week that your family buys frequently (perhaps once a week but at least once a month) and write them down in a simple notebook (this is what is known as a price book). When you are out shopping, make a point of stopping at one more shop than usual and write down the prices of your four items there; then compare them to what you have been paying at your normal one-stop store. Repeat this step each week until you have the lowest prices for at least the top 30 items you buy over and over again for your family.

Further Resources

The link to how I set up my price book is available in the resource page that goes with this book, which can be found on my blog, *Snail Pace Transformations,* at http://snailpacetranformations.com/thrifty-resources.

Thrifty People Do
Develop an Inner Clearance GPS

A thrifty person doesn't just look at clearance differently, they also seem to find it no matter where they are shopping or how they are shopping, whether online or in-store.

In-store shopping

Pretty much everyone knows that to find *Target* clearance deals you stroll by the end caps, but thrifty people know where clearance is located in every store they shop at. They seem to have blinders for all else in the store but the clearance rack.

In clothing stores it is usually towards the back or near the fitting rooms. In hardware stores it is often found on temporary racks placed in the center of the largest aisles.

Grocery stores tend to put the dry food clearance items on a rack near the employee entrance to the back of the store. The deeply-discounted produce is on a similar rack, usually tucked in a corner of the produce section. The marked-down breads are normally on a rack with wheels, either near the dairy section or floating in the middle of the bread section. These rules don't apply for all stores but for most.

There is one last area of the grocery store that thrifty people pay attention to — that is the marked-down meat. A thrifty person knows that each store seems to get their shipments of meat on the same day of the week, meaning it also expires on another day each week. When thrifty people find a marked-down meat deal, they take note of the time and day of the week that they happened to find it, and they come back to that store the same day next week, just a bit earlier. Chances are they are rewarded with not just discounted meat but a larger selection. A thrifty person will keep this up until they get there right when the meat workers are marking down the meat; then they will quickly finish up their other shopping in the store and return to the meat aisle to have the largest selection of marked-down meat possible.

This thrifty meat secret isn't 100% foolproof, but it has worked for our thrifty family with some regularity.

ONLINE STORES

Thrifty people also have a knack for finding out about online clearance sales, too. I will give away our secret: we sign up for the emails of our favorite stores. In order not to have their important, personal emails lost in a sea of their favorite store emails, thrifty people know to have two emails — one for work and family, and one for stores, freebie deals, and point programs.

It really takes just seconds to delete emails from stores when thrifty people are not hunting for their next deal, and those seconds become totally worth it when thrifty families find items on their families' shopping list that have been deeply discounted.

TIME OF YEAR

Most thrifty newbies know that the best time to shop summer clothing clearance racks is late August to early September and that the best winter clothing discounts are found in mid-to-late February. But only the more seasoned thrifty people know that there are many more times of the year to remember when it comes to getting the best clearance deals.

For instance, if you are renovating a house, a thrifty person knows that hardware stores tend to offer huge clearance deals about once a year when the models of things such as kitchen hardware, lighting, and kitchen faucets change. Around where we live, this seems to happen in the spring and sometimes again in the fall, just as it does with clothing at clothing stores.

Thrifty runners know that running shoes are like cars in that models are changed up a bit on a yearly basis. Typically this happens in January, so if you want a great deal on those running shoes you love, start looking in December or early January when running stores want the older model out of the way to make room for the new one.

If a thrifty person wants Christmas clearance items at deep prices and doesn't care too much about selection, they stay home the day after Christmas and venture out January 1st instead, when most stores will have them marked down to as much as 90% off.

Snail-Pacing Action Step

List one item you want to start getting on clearance more often, then start keeping an eye out for it. For help, search *Pinterest* for "best time to buy" guides.

Thrifty People Do
VIEW HOLIDAY CLEARANCE UNIQUELY

Thrifty people don't view the holiday clearance aisle or rack like the rest of the world does. It is because they tap into their creative thinking skills more than most. I know I have a chapter that addresses out-of-the-box thinking, but I thought how thrifty people use it to shop holiday clearance needed a chapter all its own.

Take Christmas clearance, for instance. A normal person sees it and thinks it is a great time to stock up on cards and gift wrap for next year, but here is a list of things a thrifty person starts thinking about when they see that same Christmas markdown aisle:

GIFT WRAP FOR THE WHOLE YEAR

Thrifty people look for wrapping paper, tissue paper, and gift bags that are neutral enough to use for birthdays and other occasions throughout the year.

Baking chocolate

Thrifty people stock up on Kisses and M&M's for use in baking at prices cheaper than chocolate chips. They don't mind that they are Christmas colors. Chocolate is chocolate.

Kitchen and bed linens

Thrifty people snatch up plain red flannel sheet sets and white and red kitchen linens, knowing that once they are not around all the other Christmas stuff they won't scream Christmas.

Tape and packing supplies

Tape is tape, and why it is in the Christmas clearance aisle makes no sense to this thrifty gal, but it doesn't stop me from snatching up enough of it to last me the whole year through.

Gifts for giving through the year

Thrifty people know that in late January, toys for the Christmas season will drop as low as 90 percent off. Thrifty people make a list in advance of all the birthday parties their children normally get invited to and stock up, adding one additional gift for a girl and a boy just in case. If they end up not needing them, thrifty people donate them to Christmas toy drives.

Ribbon and other craft items

Thrifty people scan the markdown Christmas ribbons for colors they can use all year. They also look for yarn, buttons, and other craft supplies that aren't blatantly Christmasy.

Kitchen items

Thrifty people know cookie cutters are not the only kitchen items found marked down after Christmas. In my own thrifty life I was able to buy a glass cake stand for 75% off, just because the box it was in had snowflakes on it. I was also able to grab a huge glass trifle bowl for the same reason.

This thrifty way of looking at Christmas doesn't stop with Christmas clearance; it continues again during Valentine clearance, Easter clearance, Fourth of July clearance, and even Halloween clearance. Throughout the year, holiday clearance sales save thrifty people and their families hundreds of dollars.

Snail-Pacing Action Step

Next time you see holiday items on clearance, take a few minutes to shift your thinking from logical to creative and try to see some of the items as useful beyond the holiday they were created for.

Section Three:

Thrifty People Know

Thrifty People Know
YOU NEED THE RIGHT-SIZE SHOVEL

Truth: You can only be so thrifty. Sometimes, even if you pinch every penny until it screams, you are still not going to achieve financial independence. Depending on your current financial state, being thrifty may not be enough to get your monthly bills paid each month.

When a thrifty person is feeling financially crunched, they might spend an evening or two figuring out if they have a few holes in their budget that could be patched by learning a few new thrifty actions, but after that they are going to start spending their time looking for a bigger shovel.

What I mean by this is sometimes the answer to your financial problems isn't lowering your already almost-as-low-as-you-can-go expenses. By "almost," I mean that very few of us truly have taken our expenses as low as they could go. We cling to things like home internet and the odd takeout meal for convenience sake — and that is okay, but I think we need to be aware of it. These conveniences are a blessing, not a right; and we should view them that way. If you truly don't want to give them up, that is fine; but know that the cost is going to be working more to pay for them.

Increasing income has always been second to making current income stretch further in our household, and yet it has also been needed on a regular basis.

For our family, for the most part, we have had my husband take a second job working for another company; but I know for others their work schedule is just not regular enough to fit another job around it.

If that is your situation, here are a few things beyond going out and getting a second job that can help you earn more money each month.

7 Ways to Create A Bigger Shovel Without Gaining Another Boss

1. Resell like mad and pay off a debt

Do you have a small debt that perhaps you could knock out with a yard sale, a Craigslist blitz, or a selling frenzy in a *Facebook* buy-and-sell group? This might not take as long as you think. I have personally made $600 at one yard sale, and between June and October of this year my family was able to raise over $5000 by selling things we no longer need. That is an average of $1000 a month made by reselling.

What I am going to tell you to do with the money goes against all debt snowball rules... Ready? Use the money to pay off your smallest debt, and then don't roll all of the payment savings into the next smallest debt.

Instead, use a percentage of it (say 10 to 15 percent) to give yourself some budget breathing room. So if the debt that you knocked out had a $100 payment each month, you would add $10 to $15 to your monthly budget and then roll the other $85 to $90 into paying down the next debt faster.

Yes, I know that goes against all the rules that debt-free gurus chant over and over, but for people on a small income this can (in my opinion) inspire you to pay off more debts faster than putting 100% on the next debt.

Why? Because people on small incomes may be looking at years or close to a decade of peanut butter sandwiches with the 100% snowball plan if their debts are high. This way you get the reward of a turkey sandwich once in awhile along the journey to becoming debt free, and you haven't increased the timeline all that much.

Seeing extra money in the spending budget each month can be just the incentive a family on a small income needs to push themselves to earn more and pay off debts faster. They start feeling the positive effects of more wiggle room in the budget right away.

Once you feel like you have enough breathing space in the budget (say you can now afford meat in all your sandwiches), stop taking from the snowball with the next debt payoff and return to the 100% snowball plan.

2. Sell other people's stuff

When I used to do *eBay* and *Craigslist* on a fairly consistent basis, I would have friends ask me if I would sell their stuff and charge them a fee. I never did feel confident enough at my re-selling skills to take them up on their offers; but if you do, then I say go for it. Spend some time researching online about what to charge and how to set up a good system before jumping in.

3. Sell a product locally

Do you make cupcakes everyone raves about? Find out what you need to do legally in your area to sell them to others.

Do you make dog biscuits that drive the dogs at the local dog park wild? See if the pet stores in your area will sell them for you.

4. Start a service-oriented business

Walk dogs in your area. Mow grass. Weed flower beds. Clean windows. These type of jobs are more flexible than working for someone else because you are in charge of setting the hours.

5. Sell your products or service online

If you love to craft, sell your products on *Etsy*; or you can open up a shop on *Shopify*. I know there are both pros and cons to each of these major craft-selling platforms, so I would suggest spending time researching both first and then choosing the one that suits your needs best.

If you are a teacher and you make up printable products for your class already, try selling them at *Teachers Pay Teachers. Teachers Pay Teachers* is a website where teachers can buy printable resources from other teachers. Sellers must provide at least one free product, but the rest of your products can be sold at a cost.

Are your pictures amazing? Perhaps you could sell them to stock photo companies. Simply enter a search into Google that says something like "where to sell stock photos" and you should find plenty of help to get you started.

If you are talented in photo editing, or editing essays, or another type of service that can be provided online, then look into getting started on *Fiverr*. *Fiverr* is what I would describe as a digital odd-job platform. You can offer your services starting at $5 to people who need them. There appears to be a bit of a learning curve to it; so again, as with any other selling platform I have suggested, I would recommend researching the best way to set up and start on *Fiverr* before you begin.

6. Fill in small cracks of time with filling out surveys and participating in point programs

I am lumping survey companies and point programs together because they are both ways to make a small income in little moments here and there throughout your day.

Survey programs are fairly simple to explain — you set up an account, and you fill out surveys. Some survey companies are more fruitful than others, and I make it part of my job at *Snail Pace Transformations* to try them out and share with my readers only the ones worth working for. You can visit the resources page for this book at http://snailpacetranformations.com/thrifty-resources/ for links to the ones I recommend.

"Point programs," to be honest, might be a term I made up — but if I did, it is one I have been using for years, and no one has called me out on it. What I consider to be point programs are programs that offer "points" in exchange for your completing tasks, filling out surveys, shopping online through their links, and more. You can exchange these points for gift cards, or in some cases *PayPal* deposits, when you reach a certain point cashout threshold.

For the most part, I prefer point programs over survey sites, because they offer so many different ways to earn. Therefore it is easier to hit the cashout limits than it is with most survey companies.

I earned $50 a month regularly combining point programs and surveys when my kids were little, and I really never spent more than 3 or 4 hours a week at it. In those hours I was also working on something else, too. That was over 10 years ago, and since then many new programs have popped up. I now believe it is possible to earn $100 a month by combining survey programs with various point programs.

To make survey companies and point programs the most profitable, you don't want to be spending hours you could be using to earn a greater return for your time. Instead use them for tasks you already do online or do tasks for them in those moments of time you can't fill with paid work.

Here is what I mean. Point programs often have a search reward function, meaning if you download their search engine and use it, you get points for searching the web — something you already do. These companies also often have apps where you could do tasks for points while standing in line. As for surveys, fill them out at the end of the day when your brain is just too tired for any other type of work.

For a list of point programs I have used and like, visit the resource page for this book that I mentioned in the survey section above.

7. Buy items for resale

Whether it be yard sale items to list on *eBay* or clearance-found items to sell on *Amazon*, buying to resell can bring in a nice sum of money each and every month.

8. Start a blog

Blogging is not a fast money-maker. It took me two years to start earning a small, part-time income. I am currently just finishing up my fourth year of blogging and am now earning a full-time income — one that is just above minimum wage. Still, I do get to work when I want to, for the most part, and that is a huge plus for me.

There are bloggers out there that made it to full-time income at around the one year mark, but they are the exception and not the norm — and many bloggers who do earn a full-time income in a year or so time frame admit to working an insane amount of hours each week to make it happen. Blog success, and the length of time it will take you to generate a good income, also depends on your niche, the audience you attract, and your ability to learn how to market yourself and your blog well.

My advice is to start one of the other seven points above to get some income flowing right away and then start the blog and watch it grow over time.

A blog is also a great way to advertise any other work you might do. I see a lot of *Etsy* shop owners who also write a blog. I have also seen resellers start them. If you were to do this, the blog would help your main source of income grow as well as becoming an income source of its own.

Snail-Pacing Action Step

This week go through your house and list one item you no longer need but is still in good condition in a local *Facebook* buy-and-sell group and use the money to pay down a debt.

Further Resources

For a list of point programs, links to reselling, and blogging tips, visit the resource page for this book found at http://snailpacetransformations.com/thrifty-resources.

Thrifty People Know
How to Make Their Smartphone Pay

You will probably meet a thrifty person or two that is still carrying around a flip phone. However, for the most part, thrifty people have found their way into the smartphone market, thanks to the economical plans offered by companies like *Ting* and *Tracfone*. And, of course, thrifty people have found ways to make those smartphones pay.

Those that haven't made the switch probably own at least a tablet of some sort that has similar functions to a smartphone.

The list of money-saving apps and money-saving smartphone uses grows daily. It won't take long for this part of the book to get outdated. However, I still wanted to share the apps and money-saving functions of my smartphone that I love.

A SMARTPHONE CAN SAVE THRIFTY PEOPLE MONEY ON TEXTING

Textfree **(also known as Pinger):** Before I had an iPhone and before *Facebook* Messaging became so popular, I used the *Textfree* app as a way to save money on texts. The only thing I didn't like about it was I couldn't use my real cell number, so it sometimes caused my friends to stare at their phones in confusion, wondering who the text was from. To avoid this I tried to always start a new thread of conversation with "Hi, Victoria here...."

iPhone to iPhone Messaging: I love that I can text my friends with iPhones from my iPhone in wifi areas, and it doesn't eat into my text package. My iPhone lets me know who I text that doesn't have an iPhone by putting my texts to them in green whereas those to iPhones are blue.

Facebook Messaging: If my friends don't have an iPhone, I try to use the *Facebook* messaging app to contact them. Most people have this app and have it set up to notify them the same way they would get notified if they had a text.

WhatsApp: I personally have not yet used the *WhatsApp* but plan to try it out very soon. It allows you to make international calls using a wifi connection for free. It also allows you to send free texts and even do free video calling.

A SMARTPHONE SAVES THRIFTY PEOPLE MONEY ON TRANSPORTATION COSTS

Gas Buddy: *Gas Buddy* lets me see who has the best available gas prices in the town I am in when I need to fill up.

A smartphone lets a thrifty person indulge in their love of learning for free

Kindle App: I download my free *Kindle* finds to the *Kindle* app on my iPhone so I can read pretty much anywhere. I am finding I read so much more this way, because a book is always at my fingertips.

Podcasts: No matter what you want to learn, you can probably find a podcast or several about that topic. On an iPhone you can find out about podcasts you love by using the *Podcast* app provided by iTunes. Android users have several free options for listening to podcasts, including *Stitcher* and *Podcast & Radio Addict*.

YouTube: There is a *YouTube* app available for smartphones that makes videos on whatever you want to learn about more accessible.

A SMARTPHONE LETS YOU GET EVEN MORE USE OUT OF YOUR LIBRARY CARD

New apps for ebooks, audiobooks, magazines, movies, and music that are tied to your library card are coming out all the time. What one library offers might not be the same as another, so I would suggest contacting your local library first to see what apps they are a part of.

Overdrive: My library offers *Overdrive,* but in my opinion the selection of products available is poor. However, I have a friend who lives in a much larger city than I do, and when she heard me complaining about it, she was shocked. She opened up her *Overdrive* app for me and I was then the one that had that surprised look on her face. The app in her area was offering four times the selection than it was in mine. In conclusion, I think it is safe to say your experience with the *Overdrive* app will depend on your location.

Hoopla: This is the app I use most often. I use it mostly for audiobooks and music. The only bummer is the current six titles per month limit. I also can't seem to figure out how long you get each type of media. My ebooks seem to stay available longer than the music. The selection is amazing in *Hoopla*, which is why it is my favorite.

OneClickDigital: My library currently does not offer *OneClickDigital,* so I can only write about what I have heard from others; and that is that it has a good selection of products available.

A SMARTPHONE SAVES THRIFTY PEOPLE MONEY ON GROCERIES AND OTHER PURCHASES

Links for signing up for all the various apps below can be found at the resource page for this book at http://snailpacetransformations.com/thrifty-resources.

Ibotta: A rebate app that offers rebates for clothing, pet care supplies, movie tickets, food, and much more.

Receipt Hog: A fun and simple app that gives you rebates back by uploading your receipts from grocery stores and more.

BerryCart: Although I personally don't use *BerryCart* much, I want to mention it, as it offers a lot of gluten-free items for rebates. I know that is a health issue for many, and gluten-free items can be expensive; so any way to save on them is appreciated.

Checkout 51: A great app that will save you money on your groceries, no matter where you shop.

Shopkick: This is really more of a money-earning app than a money-saving one, but I use it most often when I enter the doors of the places I shop for groceries. You simply open the app when you head inside the store, and it will give you points. You get more points when you scan certain items as you shop (of course this uses data or wifi).

MobiSave: You can use *MobiSave* wherever you shop. It always seems to have a small assortment of non-brand-specific deals. My favorite part about *MobiSave,* though, is that there is no minimum cash-out threshold — meaning that even if you claim just one .25 rebate, you get your rebate deposited into your *Paypal* account generally within 24 hours.

A SMARTPHONE MAKES LOSING WEIGHT FOR FREE EASIER

Lose It App: There are many free calorie-counting apps out there, and I have tried a few, but I like the Lose It app best. It is simple to use and helps you track calories in and out.

Weight Loss Coach by Fooducate: This app not only tracks calories, but it rates the food you are eating. This app is great for those trying to eat healthier foods with less junk.

Workout Trainer/Personal Fitness Coach: If you are looking for a way to work out for free, the Workout Trainer app has thousands of free videos available.

Workout Tracker By JEFIT: This app is for those who wish to pursue strength training or bodybuilding. It has 1300+ exercises to try and detailed instructions about each one.

All Trails: If you are a hiker, this app looks like it would help you get out there and hike more, no matter where you are. It contains trail maps for more than 50,000 trails across North America.

OTHER HANDY FUNCTIONS OF A SMARTPHONE THAT THRIFTY PEOPLE LOVE

Camera: A camera in your pocket is great for taking pictures of the kids, but thrifty people love it for more than that. I have used mine to help compare prices from store to store on major items I am saving up for. It is also great for storing wish list items that you see and want but don't really need. This has stopped me from many an impulse buy. I simply snap a picture and tell myself I will think about it, and rarely do I actually go back and buy the item.

Notes Area: One of the most used areas of my iPhone is the *Notepad* app. There I write myself notes such as what sizes of clothing the children currently wear or the measurements of the area that I want to find a table for. These notes help me out when I find a good yard sale or clearance find.

New money-saving apps are popping up all the time. I find out about most of the ones I use from friends, fellow bloggers, and *Pinterest.*

SNAIL-PACING ACTION STEP

Look for one app that you can download to your phone that will save you money. Start using it; and when you are in the habit of using it regularly, download another.

Thrifty People Know
NOT TO GO DIRECTLY TO THE WEBSITE

When a thrifty person wants to order something online, they are not going to just click over to the website that sells the item they want and order it.

Instead they go through a process of steps to make sure they are getting an item of value at a great price.

READ THE REVIEWS

First, if they haven't purchased the item before, they are going to take some time to research it. I talk more about how thrifty people research in the chapter "Thrifty People Are Researchers" in part one of this book. Here, however, are a few general questions thrifty people ask: Is the product as good as they think it is? Does it hold up over time? Is the customer service satisfactory?

After deciding the purchase is well worth it, they are then going to start figuring out how they can save money on it.

Search or wait for a sale

If the item isn't already on sale, a thrifty person is going to figure out just how long they can wait for it to go on sale. They then sign up for the company's emails so they are alerted to such a sale.

Search for a cash back

A thrifty person is a member of many cashback sites and sites offering points as a type of cashback. By signing up for several different point programs and cashback sites, thrifty families increase their odds of finding a discount or a point reward to give them a deeper discount than just a sale alone. A selection of cashback sites also lets a thrifty person compare values of cashbacks being offered, since every percentage off is more money that stays in a thrifty person's wallet.

For a complete list of the cashback sites I recommend, check out the resource page for this book at http://snailpacetransformations.com/thrifty-resources.

Search for discount codes

Thrifty people love *Retailmenot.com* for its great selection of discount codes, free shipping codes, and its easy-to-search website.

Search for coupons

From reading *MoneySavingMom.com,* our thrifty family finds out about free magazine subscriptions to popular magazines such as *Good HouseKeeping* and *Better Homes & Gardens.* Inside those free magazines are coupons for various stores that can be used online as well as in-store.

Search for discounted gift cards

Cardpool is currently my family's favorite online discount gift card site, but there are other companies out there offering discounted gift cards.

Our family keeps a selection of these cards on hand at all times for the stores we shop at most, so we can use them whenever we see a good sale and save an additional percentage off. Sometimes we are able to snag these cards at as much as a 20% discount.

I talk more about how our family uses discounted gift cards in the chapter "Thrifty People Know Gift Cards Are Not Just For Gift-Giving."

Search point program accounts for possible gift card cashouts

This sometimes take a bit of thinking ahead, since most of the time point program gift cards take days to weeks to be delivered; but it can be a great way to save.

Of course, there are some point programs that offer either instant or within 24-hour delivery of gift cards, such as *instaGC* and *PrizeRebel*. At *instaGC* you get your gift cards instantly — plus cashouts for *Amazon* begin at just $1. At *PrizeRebel,* once you have reached diamond level you get an instant *Amazon* gift card payment that starts at just $3.

If our thrifty family is about to place an order on *Amazon,* these are the point reward accounts where I go to check balances before placing my order. I might only be able to get a few dollars from either source, but every little bit adds up.

Search for referral credits

When my thrifty family finds a site offering a great deal that we like, we don't keep the secret to ourselves; we share it with our friends on social media and now on my blog.

Often, we are rewarded by the company with referral credits that can be used towards purchases on their sites.

The golden rule of referral credits for thrifty people is only share deals that are so great you would share them even if you didn't receive some reward for it.

Search for daily deals

Sometimes daily deal sites like *Groupon* or *LivingSocial* will offer daily deals on items thrifty people are planning to buy or for stores they are planning to shop at. When this happens, thrifty people pick up these deals and try to use them with as many of the steps above as possible.

These are nine steps thrifty people take before heading to the website to purchase, but there is one last step thrifty people also do — and it is the most important one. Before even starting the first step, thrifty people ask, "Do I really even need this?" And that ends up reducing the need to take all the other steps 9 times out of 10.

Snail-Pacing Action Step

You might be looking at this list, and all these steps are new to you, and your mind is spinning at so many steps to remember — but you don't have to do all these steps on every online purchase starting from this day forward. Instead, pick one that you think would make the biggest impact on your budget and would be fairly simple to start doing, such as using cashback sites. When you are remembering to use them most of the time, pick another, and so on. The key is making each a habit so they become second nature. That will reduce the amount of time to implement them all.

How to Shrink the Price at the Store By Stacking the Savings

There are people that find a deeply discounted item and shout for joy — then there are thrifty people. Thrifty people find the discounted item and start thinking, "How can I push the price even lower?"

They combine thrifty practices talked about in various chapters of this book to take the deal and make it a steal of a deal.

The last chapter talked about how thrifty people do this online; this chapter focuses on how thrifty people do this at brick-and-mortar stores.

AN EXAMPLE OF HOW I USED THESE PRINCIPLES TO BUY SOME YARN

I sold dishcloths I had already knitted to a friend of a friend. I knit only a small handful of patterns and my favorite is that of a dishcloth. I give many away but I also

193

sell just enough to keep me in yarn. That way my hobby costs my family zero.

I bought a discounted gift card to JoAnn's. *JoAnn's* sells my favorite type of yarn at a good price. Since this is where I shop, I keep my eyes peeled at *Cardpool* for their sales on *JoAnn's* cards, regularly getting them for up to 17% off.

I saved even more by applying a referral credit. Since I have been happy with the service my family has received from *Cardpool,* I talk about them on my blog, sharing referral links when I do. Each time people use those links to save money for their family, I get a referral credit that I can apply to my next order.

I shopped the clearance rack. *JoAnn's* was clearing out the summer colors of my favorite yarn when I visited the store. This meant my yarn was marked down by 50%.

I used a coupon. A few times per year, *JoAnn's* will send out a coupon with which you can save so much off your entire purchase, and the amount you save depends on how big your purchase is. These are one of the rare coupons that you can use on sale items. I did a thrifty dance when I figured out I could use it this time.

Count it up! I stacked six ways to save on top of one another to drop the price of my yarn purchase down as low as possible.

Snail-Pacing Action Step

Next time you have a purchasing need, don't just wait for it to go on sale, but think about how you can stack savings — so that when it does go on sale, you, too, can change a deal into a steal of a deal.

Thrifty People Know
to Look for Coupons Everywhere

Most people know to look in the Sunday paper or go to a printable coupons site for a coupon before shopping, but thrifty people go way beyond those two places when looking for a coupon.

A FEW PLACES THRIFTY PEOPLE LOOK FOR DISCOUNTS THAT YOU MIGHT NOT HAVE THOUGHT ABOUT

1. Free magazines

I love it when I can subscribe to magazines through completely free offers usually found on one of my favorite money-saving sites, *Money Saving Mom*. Honestly, I don't read all the free magazines that come in my mailbox, but you can be certain of one thing: I flip through each page looking for coupons. Magazine coupons have saved me money on dinners out, clothing, home decor purchases, food, personal products, and much more.

Coupons can be found in magazines either as a tear out or on the actual pages of the magazine itself. Don't forget to also look for coupon codes that you can use to save money on online purchases.

2. Email clubs

I have an email address set up just for email clubs. To avoid email overload, I sign up for emails just from stores our family uses most often. For instance, currently we purchase a lot of the clothes our teenagers wear from *Old Navy*, so I signed up to receive emails from *Old Navy*.

Old Navy and other stores send out special, email subscriber only, printable coupons or coupon codes to be used online and in-store. Often (but not always) these coupons can be combined with sales and clearance items, sweetening my savings.

3. Junk mail

In our town the postman delivers a great big stack of what most think is junk mail about once a month. Truly, most of it is junk mail; but buried in that pile I have found coupons for my favorite low-price grocery store, *Aldi* (yep even *Aldi* gives out the occasional coupon), as well as coupons for locally-owned restaurants and chain restaurants. Our family has also used coupons for oil changes and tire rotations that we have found in these stacks of junk mail.

4. Receipts

Often when I pop into *Family Dollar* to pick up something, I will find a $5 off $25 printable coupon at the bottom of the receipt. In another town certain stores have coupons for other stores in the area printed on the backs of their receipts.

5. Free samples

Free samples often come with high-value coupons. Some of these coupons can be used to purchase the travel-size product found in stores for either free or just pennies. Two great sources for finding out about free sample offerings are the blogs *Money Saving Mom* and *Freebies4Mom*.

6. In store

In a hardware store we frequent, they keep a bulletin board full of coupons near their service desk. In other stores our family finds coupons on the actual packages of the items we are buying or stuck on the shelf the products are on. In gas stations I often see coupons up at the cash register area. Other times, once you've purchased an item, the store will give you a coupon good on your next purchase.

7. Coupon apps

You don't necessarily need a smartphone to use a coupon app; all you need is a tablet of some sort with a camera (preferably rear-facing) to upload the receipt with. My chapter on making your smartphone pay listed the coupon apps I use.

8. Online coupon code sites

Retailmenot is probably the most popular site for online coupon codes and for good reason. I find their site to be simple to use and their codes to be the most up-to-date, and I have tried out several other sites.

9. Special Event Goodie Bags

If you have entered a local race or have gone to a conference or local event, chances are you got a bag full of goodies; and usually in those goodies are a few coupons for items you might use, restaurants in the area, or services that you might need.

10. Inside the product itself

Sometimes, instead of putting a coupon on the outside of the box, a manufacturer will put it inside the packaging. A brand of tea I like did this for years (sad day when they stopped appearing for this thrifty, tea-drinking gal).

11. Cashback sites

I am noticing more and more that cashback sites are offering coupons — either printable or as an online code — in addition to the usual cashbacks on their sites.

12. On business *Facebook* pages or other social media sites

Brands or local businesses even offer their *Facebook* or other social media fans special printable coupons or coupon codes through a status update link or as part of the status itself.

I follow a few brands that I love that are known to do this on *Facebook,* and to make sure I don't miss out on these deals, I click on the "get notifications" tab on their *Facebook* page.

Snail-Pacing Action Step

I have listed twelve places to find coupons beyond the Sunday paper and printable coupon sites. The idea of looking twelve new places for coupons can be overwhelming, so instead I suggest picking just one place to look for now. Choose the one option that you think would be the easiest to make a habit, as that is the one that will end up saving you the most money.

When you get in the habit of using that source for coupons, pick another source and make it a habit. Repeat over and over, and soon you will be looking all twelve places, just like a thrifty ninja does.

Thrifty People Know
THAT LOYALTY CAN BE REWARDING

From time to time a thrifty person will come across a brand they love. They might fall in love because of the quality or price of the product or the customer service the brand offers. It might also be that they just love the taste of the product or the atmosphere of the brand.

When this sort of brand romance develops, thrifty people are going to check and see just how they can keep their new love as inexpensive as possible. One way they do this is to see if the brand has a loyalty program.

There are several places a thrifty person will search for a brand loyalty program.

THE PRODUCT PACKAGING

The first place the thrifty person checks for a brand loyalty program is on the box itself. For instance, my husband loves *Coke-a-Cola*, and on their boxes one day years ago I saw the *Mycokerewards* symbol. When I entered it into a search engine online, it directed me to *Mycokerewards.com*. There I was able to sign up and start earning points for purchasing coke products that I could then cash in for magazine subscriptions, photobooks, gift cards, and more.

The cash register

Often the sales associate at the cash register will alert me to a loyalty program the store has. You have to be careful with these offers, as some come as part of a store credit card signup; or they are available for a price. Rarely do either of these situations turn out to be a thrifty deal. However sometimes the loyalty program is tied to nothing but your purchases, and those are the ones I jump on. This is how I found out about the *McAlister's Tea* card and the *MyPanera* club.

Store signage

Thrifty people take a second to look around the store to skim the signage found on the store's walls and door as they walk in. These are often the places stores will promote loyalty programs that thrifty people will ask a sales associate about.

Cash Receipts

Sometimes companies will advertise the website where you can sign up for their loyalty program at the bottom of everyone's cash receipt.

Word of mouth

Thrifty people love sharing thrifty deals. I am always sharing different loyalty programs with my friends when I see them shopping at a store that has one, or eating at a restaurant with one, or buying a product from a brand that has one.

Stickers on gift cards

A big thrifty beef of mine is when I give people a *Starbucks* gift card as a gift, and then the first thing I see is the recipient peeling off the sticker telling them about the *Starbucks Rewards* program and tossing it in the garbage.

I want to scream "I gave you that gift card because I know you love Starbucks; don't you care that there is a way to save money on your expensive yet addicting coffee?" After all, you get a free drink just for registering the card and another one on your birthday; that is two free coffees that you didn't even have to purchase anything to get.

Thrifty websites

Blogs that share deals or money-saving tips will often share loyalty programs with their readers.

WEBSITE SEARCHES

Enter the name of your favorite brand, store, or restaurant into your favorite search engine and chances are a website will come up that you can visit. At the website, search for a loyalty program or perhaps instead a birthday club program or email list that you can sign up for. These programs will often give you free items, discount codes, and coupons towards your vice.

Of course the trick to keeping loyalty programs truly rewarding is to make sure that you are not buying more of that particular product or visiting that store or restaurant more often than you normally would, just so that you can enjoy their free bonuses more often.

Loyalty programs are only rewarding if you keep to your regular buying frequencies and just cash in on the rewards whenever you happen to earn one. Visiting *Starbucks* twice a week instead of your normal once a week, just so you can get to the free cup of coffee reward twice as fast, is not thrifty. However, continuing to visit *Starbucks* once a week with a friend so that you and she can catch up on each other's lives and taking advantage of the *Starbucks Rewards* card while you are there — that is being a wise, thrifty steward.

Snail-Pacing Action Step

Pick one restaurant your family eats at frequently, or a store you shop at frequently, or a brand you buy often. Take a few moments this week to figure out if they offer some type of loyalty program by looking at the places I mentioned above. Repeat this over and over, and soon you will be cashing in on some pretty great rewards for your loyalty. Just remember: don't let the promise of free items change your buying frequency.

Thrifty People Know

GIFT CARDS ARE NOT JUST FOR GIFT-GIVING

People often think that gift cards can only be used as gifts and can only be bought at face value. Thrifty people know that simply isn't true. Our thrifty family saves as much as $300 a year by buying discount gift cards. That is a savings of $25 a month, and we don't take advantage of this thrifty practice as much as we could. If we were more diligent and thought ahead more often, we could probably easily double that savings.

Our family uses *Cardpool* to buy our discounted gift cards. There are other discounted gift card companies out there, but *Cardpool* is what we stick to as they have been around the longest, while other companies we have used have come and gone.

You can purchase gift cards for a small handful of restaurants and other services at a discount at *Costco*; but you do need a membership for *Costco*, and you need to buy a high dollar value of one type of gift cards at one time. At *Cardpool*, our thrifty family buys gift cards that start at around $25.

Another way to get discounted gift cards is to take advantage of the Christmas "buy $50 in gift cards, get $10 free" deals you see for businesses you frequent. These deals will get you discounts on cards that the discounted sites might not carry; but they are found primarily only at Christmas time, whereas discounted gift card deals at sites like *Cardpool* are found all year long.

One last source of discounted gift cards that just came on my radar recently is a site called *MyGiftCardPlus*. The site works with *Swagbucks* to offer its customers SB points back with every purchase instead of a discount. Essentially you have to wait for your money back, but you don't have to wait more than 24 hours for your electronically delivered gift card code. However, even though my family loves everything *Swagbucks*, we are still sticking to *Cardpool* because a certain member of the family loves hold-in-your-hand-gift cards over the print-out type — but I still love the "can you enter that code for me; I don't know how" man that he is.

Discounted gift cards are available for restaurants, clothing stores, department stores, hardware stores, and even craft stores, making them a great way to save anywhere from 2 percent to as much as 25 percent off your purchase, with no need for a sale. Of course if the item is on sale, you can still pay with your discounted gift card and essentially receive a double-dip discount — a huge thrifty thrill.

THE TRICK TO MAKING DISCOUNTED GIFT CARDS REALLY WORK FOR YOUR BUDGET IS TO ALWAYS THINK AHEAD.

For instance, when we get into the discounted gift card groove — and I wish we would more often — we get out our calendar and think about expenses that we will have starting around three weeks out and for the next four weeks after that. We think that far ahead because it does take awhile to get the physical gift cards in the mail; although, as I mentioned, there are printable gift cards that take just 24 hours or less to receive.

We might decide we want to book a date night, so we will search for what gift cards are available at *Cardpool* for restaurants in our area. Perhaps we figure out that we will finally have time to start that renovation project; if so we will take the time to figure out what it is going to cost us and then order a gift card for *Home Depot* for 8.5% off or *Lowes* for 7% off.

We always try to make the gift cards total 10-15% less than we think we will spend so that we don't end up with a stack of gift cards with just a few dollars on them. For example, if dinner at Chili's is going to cost us $30, we will try to get a card for $25.

Thrifty blinders are necessary when using discounted gift cards as a way to save money. That *American Eagle Outfitters* card might look tempting since it is available at 24% off, but if you don't shop there with any regularity, then chances are that particular gift card, even if it is available at a great discount, is not a good fit for you.

Stick to buying gift cards for stores you know and love and visit on a regular basis (I would say at least once a season, but once a month is better).

Also, when spending a gift card, people tend to often have the attitude that it is found money, since gift cards make us think "gift." When buying them regularly as a way to save money, this attitude has to go. Otherwise you won't help your budget out at all, but hurt it.

One last tip for using discounted gift cards the thrifty way is to make sure you put the gift cards in your wallet so you will use them. If they are the printable type, make sure you print them out the day you receive them and keep them all in one easily accessible spot. That way your gift cards don't get buried in your inbox or forgotten in a clutter pile in your home.

Physical gift cards fit well in wallets, but printable ones are awkward. If the printable gift cards are not going to be used online, I suggest devoting one area in your purse to them and perhaps storing them in a ziplock bag so they are safe from spills. If you are using them online, you can either make a folder for them in your inbox so that they don't get buried or print them out and put them in a binder or folder that is devoted to just printable gift cards.

I am noticing that many discounted gift card sites, including *Cardpool,* are now offering smartphone apps with app-friendly gift cards, which means the problem of making sure you have them with you when you shop is already beginning to be much less of a problem.

Snail-Pacing Action Step

Check out *Cardpool* or *MyGiftCardPlu*s and purchase just one gift card for a store or restaurant you frequent regularly. Once you have gone through the process of buying and using a discounted gift card once and have decided you love the extra savings they provide, do it again, but remember to buy wisely.

Further Resources

For links to discounted gift card companies, check out the resource page for this book found on my blog, *Snail Pace Transformations*, at http:// snailpacetransformations.com/thrifty-resources.

Thrifty People Know

How to Use Daily Deal Sites Wisely

Thrifty people know that daily deal sites can be a huge money saver — or a huge money and time waster. Armed with this knowledge, thrifty families set out to make sure that daily deals are used as weapons for slashing expenses rather than slashing a hole in their pockets.

Our thrifty family has used daily deal finds to cut the cost of essentials such as shampoo, vitamins, and groceries by as much as half.

We have also used daily deals to save money on less essential items, such as entertainment; and that is when we really need to be cautious to make sure we are not wasting money.

Questions a thrifty person asks themselves before buying a daily deal

1. Is this item something that I already have in the budget?

2. Can I fit the activity-based daily deal in our calendar with lots of time to spare?

Our family does have a small weekly budget that I take out in cash for entertainment and eating out purposes. If I find a daily deal for either a restaurant or for an activity we like doing as a family, such as ice skating, I will buy it; but only if we can fit the event on our calendar with lots of time to spare. I then take that much less out in cash the following week for entertainment. Since we budget ahead, we have the cash to cover the daily deal in our account, even though entertainment is a cash item in our budget.

SOME MORE TIPS ON USING DAILY DEALS

I prefer having the daily deals sent to an email address I keep separate from my work and our family's personal email address. I scan through them in little moments here and there, like while waiting in line, or waiting for my son's soccer practice to finish. If I don't have time to look at them that day, or I am really not looking for anything that might come up in a daily deal, I simply send them all to trash without even opening them.

I know I could get daily deals in app form, but I think I would forget to look at them for weeks at a time if I did; so I would probably miss out on ones that would be money-savers for our family.

Another great way to save with daily deals is to take advantage of the referral options. Some offer a set amount for every new customer you bring in; others will offer you a free deal if you share the one you purchase and a certain amount of people use your link to purchase it.

Don't spam your friends with daily deals every day; simply share those you know they will love. For instance, if your friend's favorite restaurant is offered at a daily deal site, share the link with him or her, but don't send that friend the entire list of daily deals each day.

One more way to save additional money on daily deals is to make sure you buy them through a cashback site. First I see what I want in the email the daily deal site sends me; then I go to a cashback site that I know offers cashback on purchases made at that daily deal site. To purchase my daily deal, I use the link to the daily deal site provided by the cashback site instead of the one in the email. This doesn't earn me more than perhaps $1 or so, and sometimes less; but when I do it with each and every daily deal I buy, the savings start to add up.

A list of a few of our family's favorite daily deal sites

Zulily — great for name-brand clothing deals (I like the workout clothing deals)

Groupon — we mostly use *Groupon* for ice skating and restaurant deals

LivingSocial — *LivingSocial* often runs deals on my family's favorite brand of shampoo and also on *Lucky Vitamin*, where we buy our supplements.

SNAIL-PACING ACTION STEP

Next time you are tempted by a daily deal, refer to the two thrifty questions to ask yourself. If you can't say "yes" to both, then delete the daily deal email and save your money.

FURTHER RESOURCES

For links to daily deal sites mentioned above, plus new ones I find, visit the resource page for this book found at http://snailpacetransformations.com/thrifty-resources.

Thrifty People Know
How to Shop Secondhand Wisely

Thrifty people shop secondhand, but only when it makes sense. I know some of you are thinking, "What do you mean thrifty people shop secondhand when it makes sense? I thought thrifty people always shop secondhand? After all, doesn't shopping secondhand always save you money?"

It is true that secondhand shopping can save you a significant amount of cash. However, thrifty families know there are a few times when it makes more financial sense to buy new. They buy these new items on sale, of course, and by stacking many thrifty practices on top of each other to get the price down as far a possible.

Which items each thrifty family decides to buy new instead of secondhand are going to vary from thrifty family to thrifty family, depending on their talents and abilities to fix, refinish, and repurpose items.

Sometimes new means less operating costs

In our family, for instance, we prefer to buy new appliances. We find that new appliances have greater energy efficiency, which keeps their month-to-month cost down lower than their secondhand counterparts.

Plus there is less chance of a new appliance needing a repair right away; and if it does, it is usually covered under warranty for at least one year. Parts can be costly, and if a repairman is required to do the repair, the labor can often add up to ¼ the price of buying a new appliance — and that is just for a single repair.

Sometimes new costs the same as secondhand over time

Another problem with secondhand is that it can often be a bit of a gamble as to how long the item will continue to last. Our family has learned the hard way that used appliances are sometimes being sold for a reason — they are on their last legs. You might be able to find a used stove for $100 that lasts a year, or you could buy a new one for $500 and have it last 5 years. Either way, the yearly cost of the stove is the same; but the thrifty family who bought the new stove went shopping just once, while the secondhand shoppers went shopping five times. You can complete some pretty significant projects around the house in the time it takes to shop for a stove four extra times.

Then again, you could also buy a $100 stove and have it last for 5 years; hence the reason I said buying used is a bit of a gamble. The gambling element can be lessened by being an informed buyer. Before you pick up that $100 stove, find out the reliability of the brand. How long are they known to last for? What are some common things that can go wrong with them? How much is it to fix those common problems? How much is a new model? What is the month-to-month cost to run the old versus the new model?

Sometimes new costs less right from day one

Another reason why my thrifty family has bought new instead of used is that we have found that often we can find new items for less than used ones.

For instance, this happens often to me with clothing items at consignment stores or even the odd thrift store. I see jeans of the same brand I just bought my kids new, at the same price I just paid for new by waiting for a sale and using a discount gift card and adding in an online discount code.

Despite all these reasons, though, buying secondhand still makes sense for a lot of items a family uses, in order to keep expenses low. Items such as real wood furniture that have already lasted through one family and will keep providing years of use at a fraction of the cost of new (and often better quality than new) are some of my favorite finds.

My family also considers how much we will use the item. If we are purchasing an item we are only going to use a handful of times, recouping the cost of new might not be possible. In that case it makes more financial sense to buy a used item with enough life left in it to serve our needs.

Places to find secondhand items

My absolute favorite source for secondhand finds are yard sales, where items go for as low as one-tenth of the cost of their new counterparts, and sometimes even less.

Locally owned thrift stores hold great treasures and amazing prices and often have good sales, too. I find local thrift stores in general to have better prices than nationally owned thrift stores.

However, I do go to nationally owned thrift stores, especially when I am looking for a specific clothing item for myself; and that is because of the sheer volume of items in these stores. Since these big-box type secondhand stores often have hundreds of a particular item like shirts, skirts, and jeans, there is a greater likelihood that they will have those size 8 tall skinny jeans you want for your trip that begins this weekend than the smaller thrift store near you. You will probably pay more than you would for them at a smaller thrift store, but you will still pay less than new.

Other great sources of secondhand goods are *Craigslist*, *Facebook* buy-and-sell groups, *Freecycle*, and local newspapers. You can also put a shout out on *Facebook* such as, "Our family wants to buy a _____; does anyone have one they want to get rid of?" Sometimes this results in just what you wanted for less than you figured you would spend, or you could find that someone will be willing to just let you borrow the item or trade it for something you have that they want, or they might even make it free if you are willing to pick it up from them.

Snail-Pacing Action Step

The next time you want to just go to the store and buy new, ask yourself if it would make more financial sense to buy this item used.

Further Resources

For links to articles I have written that take this topic deeper, visit the resource page for this book at http://snailpacetransformations.com/thrifty-resources.

Thrifty People Know

How to Yard Sale Shop Like A Ninja

A non-thrifty person sees yard sale shopping on a Saturday afternoon as a way to socialize with friends while finding a few deals.

A thrifty person views yard sale season like a serious hunter views hunting season. The thrifty person needs to get certain items on their list to provide for their family throughout the winter, just like a hunter needs a certain amount of meat in their freezer to support their family until the next season.

The List

Before yard sale shopping season begins, I often — though not always — go through each room and make a mental or written list of all the items we need that I could find at yard sales.

I create a written list when our needs are pretty specific, such as when I was furnishing our home and needed coffee tables, book shelves, and other furniture items that had to fit in certain spots of our home. Since

225

there were measurements involved, I wrote a list and made sure to include all measurements.

When I am not looking for such size-specific items, I just keep a running mental list. For instance, this last yard sale season I made a mental note, while going through our homeschooling supplies, that we were low on binders. When I sorted the linen closet in spring I noticed that our single sheets were getting very worn and made a mental note to look for some during the upcoming yard sale season. While rummaging through my daughter's closet I discovered she didn't have a single sweatshirt that would fit come fall, so I added sweatshirts to my mental yard sale shopping list.

By the time yard sale season was over I had found enough like-new binders to fill our needs but just one pair of sheets and no sweatshirts. So I turned to other thrifty methods to find those items.

I always try to put a purchase off until after yard sale season if I can, because I find that yard sales are the cheapest source for almost any household or clothing item a family needs.

The list helps me stick to buying needs instead of wants. It also helps me hop from sale to sale quicker. I scan each sale for items on my list and move on. This reduces wasted time at one sale, being distracted by items I don't need that could cause me to miss out on the exact item I do need at another sale.

Prepping the day before yard sale shopping

There is also a certain amount of yard sale shopping prep that begins the day before you go.

This is the day I make sure I have small bills like ones and fives — not only is this a form of yard sale politeness, but it also makes it easier to ask for a discount. If you want to pay $3 for the four shirts that should be a total of $5, but you hold out a $5 bill to the seller when you ask for a discount, more than likely they will say no. Hold out $3 and then ask for the discount, and trust me, 9 times out of 10 they will take your offer.

Although currently I stick to community-wide rummages where I can hit dozens of sales within minutes, years ago when we lived in a town that just had individual sales all over the place, I would take time to plan out a route. I wanted to make sure that the route was both time efficient and fuel efficient.

Prepping the morning of yard sale shopping

The morning of the sales I like to fill a cooler with snacks and drinks. This way I am not tempted to run to the closest gas station for pop and snacks. That can really decrease the savings for the day right there.

If I am shopping for an item that needs to be a specific size, I make sure to grab my small tape measure and stick it in my purse.

I wear comfortable shoes and bring along a large empty bag so that I can park the car in one spot at the community sale and walk from sale to sale until my bag is full. Then I walk back to the car to empty the bag and move the car to the next batch of yard sales. This saves me time and hassle. Community sales can lead to really packed streets, and parking can be hard to find.

One last thing I do is switch to a smaller, crossbody-style purse that fits the essentials only. I bring just cash, my driver's license, and my cell phone. I do this so that I can wear my purse at all times, eliminating the possibility of me putting my purse down somewhere to examine an item and then forgetting to pick it back up again. If you are not as absent-minded as me, you don't need to do this step.

During yard sale shopping

While actually yard sale shopping, thrifty people talk themselves through each purchase. No, we don't talk out loud to ourselves. Instead we hold an internal conversation. "Is this item on my to-buy list?" If not, "Do I really need this item," or "Should I ask for a lower price, or is it fair?"

Thrifty people also take time to examine each item. Some people can get very excited over a 50-cent thingamabob only to take it home and discover half the pieces are missing, and therefore they just wasted 50 cents. A thrifty person is going to take the time to open boxes, check out seams on clothing, and count pieces in games, so there are no surprises when they get home.

One last thrifty yard sale tip: thrifty people will often pick up a great deal they don't need. There are two reasons for this. One: to resell it at a profit, or two: to give it to a friend who they know was looking for that exact item. Reselling yard sale items can help pay for your gas. Giving yard sale items away warms the hearts of the thrifty.

Snail-Pacing Action Step

Take some time this week to create your own yard sale shopping list. Walk through each room in your home. Open doors on closets. As you make this mental list, take note of items that are getting worn, are fewer in number than you need, or are non-existent, and add them to your list.

Further Resources

For a complete list of links to the articles I have written about yard sale shopping, visit the resource page for this book, found on my blog, *Snail Pace Transformations,* at http://snailpacetransformations.com/thrifty-resources.

Thrifty People Know
THE BEST TIME TO PURCHASE

Thrifty people are walking, talking reference guides when it comes to the best day of the week, month, or year to buy just about anything — from pizza to bedsheets.

TAKEOUT FOOD

Pizza takeout night at our house only happens on Monday and Tuesday. Why? Because those are the days our favorite takeout pizza joint holds its one-topping large pizza sale.

When the children were little, we paid attention to where kids could eat for free on certain nights. A great way to find that information nowadays is to simply enter the words "kids eat free lists" into your search engine, and dozens of such lists on different blogs will appear.

Entertainment

Our family also rarely sees movies in the theater, but when we do you can bet we will be at a showing that starts before 4pm. Why? Because that is when movie tickets are discounted.

Thrifty families also search the websites of places such as zoos and museums to see if it is cheaper to go on certain days, or if they offer a discount for pre-buying the tickets online.

Clothing

Thrifty people know that if you want winter clothes, you should go shopping in February when the clothes are discounted to as low as 90 percent off. If you want summer clothes, then September is the time to go.

Holiday items

Thrifty people know that if you want amazing deals on holiday clearance, you don't go the day after the holiday. Instead you wait until a week after. By then it will all be 75% to 90% off, and there will still be a good selection.

Seasonal items

If a thrifty person needs hats and gloves for their family, they will try to make do with the odd assortment they have until March, when hats and gloves and other winter items begin to be deeply discounted. Summer items such as beach towels and beach toys are bought in late September.

I could keep listing the lowest time to buy everything, but thankfully, others already have. Google "the best time to buy...," filling in the blank with whatever it is you need to purchase, and you are going to find articles written by other thrifty writers that can help you out.

Snail-Pacing Action Step

Take 15 to 20 minutes searching for "the best time to buy" articles online for items that your family uses most often. If takeout is a big expense in your family, you might want to search places kids eat for free instead.

Thrifty People Know
It Pays to Keep Their Eyes Open

Thrifty people know to keep their eyes open for great sales, amazing deals, and coupons — but in this chapter, I am talking about how thrifty people always have their eyes open for new ways to save.

Each and every month, it seems, my thrifty family finds a new way to save. Perhaps a new discounted gift card site or app starts up — or a new coupon app, a new daily deal site, a new point rewards program — or a new discount store opens up.

The new never stops. There is always some new way to save on items that we need or want for our family.

6 Places Where Thrifty Families Find New Ways To Save

Friends, Family, and Coworkers: I have one friend in particular that seems to find out about great thrifty websites before I do, and I love it when she shares them with me.

My husband's coworkers know I write about all things thrifty every Friday on my blog, so when they find something new that is saving them money, they tell him about it and remind him to tell me so I can share it with my blog readers.

Social Media: I have found out about a lot of great thrifty resources from other thrifty *Facebook* friends that have shared them on *Facebook*.

Sometimes when I scroll through my Instagram feed, a fellow Instagrammer will be showing off a picture of their thrifty find and will list the thrifty source of it as a link in their profile. I, of course, take the bait and check out the site for myself.

Magazines: Magazines used to be my favorite resource for finding out about all things new and thrifty, but recently some of my favorite titles for this, including *All You* and *Shop Smart,* stopped printing issues.

I continue to find out about a new thrifty thing occasionally in the magazines I do read, though.

Blogs and Websites: As a blogger, I am always reading other blogs so that I can share my fellow bloggers' content. Often I will find another blogger writing about a thrifty app or website or service I have not heard about before, and I will check it out further.

Billboards, Commercials, and other Ads: My husband does most of the driving in our family. While he drives, I knit and read billboards. I cannot count the times when these billboards have been advertising a company that sounds like it could save us money. I will quickly note the name of the company down in the note app on my smartphone to check out later.

I have also found other great thrifty sources from TV commercials or ads on other websites.

Web and *Pinterest* Searches: I know that technically *Pinterest* is considered a social media site, but in my opinion it is more of a highly visual search engine. So I am including it with web searches.

Often if our family has a big expense coming up, I will search *Google* and *Pinterest* for ways to save money on that item. Usually, though not always, I will discover a new money-saving tip during my web searches.

SNAIL-PACING ACTION STEP

Start living with eyes wide open for new thrifty sources. Set aside a small amount of time each week to research new ways to save money.

Thrifty People Know

Social Media Can Be a Gold Mine

Time management experts view social media sites as time wasters, but a thrifty person sees them as a way to save money.

Thrifty people want to share jokes and pictures of the kids just like everyone else. They also want to post every so often about items they want to sell, share good deals their friends can get in on, or ask if they can borrow something; and these things build community just as much as jokes and pictures of the kids.

Here is a list of ways my thrifty family has used our *Facebook* account to enhance our thrifty lifestyle. I know there are many other social media sites out there, and I think much of what I list could be done on other social media sites, as well, with just slight adaptions.

To see if you can borrow an item instead of buy

We all have times where we want or need an item we will only use once. Perhaps you really want to read a book series, but the library doesn't have it. In a *Facebook* status update, simply ask your friends if anyone has that book series and is willing to let you borrow it.

Proper thrifty edict means that you are also willing to lend to *Facebook* friends in need.

Save money on items we need and sell those we no longer need

Facebook buy-and-sell groups make it so simple to buy and sell items. Our family has bought half-price mulch this way and sold hundreds of dollars of items in a short amount of time in these groups.

Free items, points, and coupon codes

Various companies offer free items through their *Facebook* pages. I have gotten free coffee, free hand cream, free body wash, and more. Most of these are sample-size, but still, free is free.

If you use point programs like *Swagbucks*, often on their *Facebook* pages they will list free codes that you can enter onto their site for points.

Other companies like *Shutterfly* share coupon codes that you can enter at their site for free items like photo books (usually you must pay shipping).

Keep your Kindle stocked with free ebooks

The site *Spirit-Filled Kindle* currently keeps my *Kindle* stocked with great free and low-priced books. I have found the simplest way for me to learn about their free offerings each day is to "like" their *Facebook* page and then head over to it and press the "get notifications" tab. Each day I am now notified whenever they update their page.

Referral bonuses

If I find a new deal that I am planning on taking advantage of, and I know my friends will like it too, I will share it whether or not it is a referral link. However, if it does have a referral link, then I get to reap rewards for my thrifty share.

Since I am very selective about what I share, making sure it will truly benefit my friends, I have had only positive feedback on my sharing. People often thank me for letting them in on the deal.

For a listing of over 40 companies that offer referral incentives, visit the resource page for this book at http://snailpacetransformations.com/thrifty-resources/.

Save Money On Pay-As-You-Go Cell Phone Plans

My family uses *Tracfone* and *Ting* for our cell phone networks. Our plan is priced per text and per minute, so to save texts and minutes whenever I am at home or in a Wi-Fi hotspot, I will send non-urgent messages to my friends through *Facebook*. Some evenings a friend and I will get really chatty through our message boxes, commenting back and forth for extended periods of time, so this really does create significant savings for our family.

Snail-Pacing Action Step

What is one thing from the list above that you could start doing right away to make *Facebook* or another social media site start saving or making you money? It might be searching and joining a local *Facebook* buy-and-sell group. Perhaps you also use a pay-as-you-go cell phone plan, and you could start using *Facebook* messaging to save you money on text message fees.

Thrifty People Know
How to Give Good Gifts

I think almost all of us have gotten that gift from the cheapskate relative or friend that we think back on each and every time someone mentions that they want to slash the cost of giving gifts.

Thrifty people know, however, that you don't have to give cheapskate gifts to save money. In fact, I have been told once or twice to stop giving such big gifts, because a friend feels they can't give the same-sized gift in return.

When this happens I am quick to point out to the friend that I don't give expecting to receive, and then I tell them the price of the gift. Yes, I do actually tell them the value, as it generally makes them feel instantly better.

Usually after I tell them the price tag, their eyes pop out of their heads, and they want to know how on earth I got a gift that large for so little. Never do they tell me I am cheap.

Make a list of how many people you need to buy for

I touch on making a Christmas gift list in the next chapter. But for this chapter I want you to get out your calendar and figure out all the other events that require you to give gifts from January 1 to December 31st. List birthdays, Mother's Day, Father's Day, graduations, weddings, etc. Think through an entire twelve-month period.

List name, sex, and age only. Do not list what you want to buy or how much you want to spend. Those two items have to remain very flexible if you are going to give good gifts for less.

Create a gift bin, shelf, or closet

Find a place in your home where you can store a gift stash. In our home this is a plastic tote with a lid that is stored in the only closet we have on the main floor of our home.

If you have more storage space than I do, the gift stash can be an entire shelf or even an entire closet.

When you are thinking of what area to use, make sure it is a space that doesn't get too hot, too cold, or too dusty. You want your items to remain new until you give them.

The gift stash area is going to be vital to you saving money on gifts. Put some thought into where and how to store gifts so that the items you stash are remembered and kept in pristine condition. It won't save you money if you don't remember you bought them in the first place or if the item is damaged before you can give it.

Always think of the surprise gift-giving opportunities

You made your gift list and you found your place to stash the great low-priced gifts (that I am about to tell you about below); but before you start buying, I want you to think about one more type of gift you will need — last-minute gifts for events you didn't foresee happening.

These gifts are often the ones that break the budget more than any other, because you didn't have the time to plan ahead.

To avoid the "price ouch" these last-minute events cause you, I recommend keeping two to three generic, unassigned gifts in your gift stash at all times.

For our home this has meant having perhaps a deeply-discounted set of Legos, or maybe a Barbie found on clearance, in the gift stash in case we need a gift for a child. For adults I might have a candle or a coffee mug.

On occasion the child gifts have sat unneeded for too long, and my children's age group changes and therefore their gift needs change. When this has happened I have donated the gift to the next toy drive. So really, it was a win-win, as a family was helped, and I saved money.

The gifts for adults, however, are generally timeless; and if we don't use them throughout the year, they become really nice white elephant gifts for Christmas parties we get invited to.

KEEP YOUR EYES OPEN FOR DEEP DISCOUNTS ON GIFT ITEMS

Whenever you see a clearance area in a store with items marked 75 percent off or more, consult your gift list and pick up what is suitable for whoever is on your list — and don't forget your surprise gift list! Are the items generic enough that anyone would love them? If they are and you are low on surprise gifts, pick one or two up.

If you can, stack savings on top of the deeply-clearanced price to further sweeten the deal, such as using a cashback app if you are in-store or a cashback site if you are online.

I generally don't even touch the clearance area for gifts unless the discount is 75% or higher, because I know I can find plenty of great gifts throughout the year to fulfill my gift list needs.

However, if you are just starting out stocking your gift stash, you might not have the time to wait until you see a 75% off or higher clearance area. In that case, just pick up what you need for the next month at 25% off or more and slowly work your way up to deeper savings as you get better at thinking ahead further and further.

START WATCHING OUT FOR FREEBIES

The chapter "Thrifty People Do Love Free Items" covers where to find free items, of which many could be gift-worthy. Flip to that chapter to find out where to get great free samples, and start collecting them so that you can turn your freebies into gifts.

For a list of my favorite ways to turn freebies into gifts, go to the resource page for this book at http://snailpacetransformations.com/thrifty-resources/.

Make a DIY gift list

To give DIY gifts that are great in quality yet low in price requires implementing the thrifty strategies taught in this book as well as planning ahead. This way you can make sure that you get your supplies on sale and still have enough time to complete the gifts before you need to give them.

The key to giving inexpensive yet wonderful DIY gifts is being flexible. Sometimes you have to let the inexpensive supplies you find tell you what to make, instead of you deciding what to make and then finding the sales.

For instance, say you want to knit everyone a scarf for Christmas. You decide you want to make it out of a certain type of yarn and that you will buy it one ball at a time using the 40% off one-item coupon you get from your local craft store each month.

That sounds like a thrifty plan, but if you are in the store and notice that a pretty shade of another type of yarn is marked down to 75% off, ditch your plan and buy all you can. You can either save the difference or add to your gift. For example, perhaps people don't get just a handmade scarf, but a scarf and a bottle of luxurious hand cream you found at 90% off.

Snail-Pacing Action Step

Add finding a safe and convenient spot for a gift stash to your to do list this week. The following week sit down with your calendar and start figuring out all the gifting occasions you face each and every year besides Christmas.

Figure out what system works the best for you to carry your gift list with you whenever or wherever you shop so that you can start taking advantage of amazing sales and giving great thrifty gifts.

Thrifty People Know
to Think Christmas All Year Long

For thrifty people, Christmas planning starts the day after Christmas. Well, okay, maybe only the keenest of thrifty people begin the very next day. But most will start by at least January 1st.

And just to let you keen thrifty people know — if you wait until January 1st, the Christmas clearance items will be marked down even further. The early bird may catch the worm, but it might not be the biggest one.

Make a list of needed Christmas supplies

While you are putting away the Christmas decorations, take a moment to grab a pen and paper so you can make a list of items you will need for next Christmas. This will allow you to grab them while they are anywhere from 50% to as much as 90% off.

Things to think about adding to your list

- tape

- wrapping paper

- tissue paper

- gift bags

- mailing envelopes

- large hooks for hanging wreaths and such

- ribbon

- Christmas lights

- Christmas cards

Your list might differ from mine a bit, but use it as a guide to get you started on things that you can buy and store now that will save you money later.

Add up those bills

Sometime between Christmas and New Year's, take a few moments to add up all the costs of this year's Christmas. Not just the gifts, but also the events, the food, the cards you sent, the clothes for special activities, the extra giving you did, the extra money for the gas you used to go to all those Christmas events, and anything else related to the Christmas season.

Once you have the total, decide how you are going to save that amount before Christmas rolls around again. You can divide the total into twelve payments, pay it off in a few bigger payments, or all in one go.

For instance, in our family my husband gets paid every other week, so twice a year we get three paychecks in one month instead of two. We often use a portion of those extra paychecks to set aside for Christmas. Other years we have put our tax return away to pay for Christmas, or we have used money earned from resell items.

You could also use money earned from point reward programs such as *Swagbucks*, or rebate apps like *Ibotta*, or cashback sites like *Ebates*. These streams of income are small on their own; but when rolled together, they could easily pay for Christmas.

MAKE A LIST OF STORES YOU SHOPPED AT THIS YEAR

Write down each and every store where you remember buying Christmas gifts. Once you have that list you can then do the following steps to save even more at those stores next year.

KEEP AN EYE OUT FOR DISCOUNTED GIFT CARDS

Our thrifty family has been using discounted gift cards to shave 10% or more off our Christmas budget for the past several years. We note where we shop and how much we generally spend at that store and then start keeping our eyes out for a good discounted gift card for that store that we can use for Christmas shopping.

It does involve a bit of careful thought and planning; but it really only takes a few minutes, and the savings are well worth it.

Join email lists for these stores

You might not want to do this step until you start your Christmas shopping, especially if you like to keep your inbox as clean as possible.

As I have mentioned before, I keep a separate email box just for stores, survey companies, and point programs. That way my work and personal email inboxes are not flooded with promotions.

I join the email lists of stores we shop at most, because they give out special online discount codes or printable in-store coupons to subscribers, leading to lower purchasing costs.

In addition to your favorite stores, I would also recommend signing up for *Brad's Deal* emails or downloading the app. This is an aggregator site for the best deals on top name-brand items such as *North Face*, *Vera Bradley*, *KitchenAid*, *Nike*, and more. I sign up for *Brad's Deals* emails typically every October and then unsubscribe after Christmas.

Take note of what cashback sites or apps offer these stores

I have saved as much as 20% on a Christmas gift just by catching a good cashback deal for the store I bought it at. Make sure to reread the chapter "Thrifty People Know Not To Go Directly To The Website" for more information about how to use cashbacks to their full advantage.

Make up your gift list by no later than January 1st

A thrifty gift list is simply a list of names of people you need to shop for and their ages and sex. It will also have a price range for the amount you want to spend on each person.

What a thrifty gift list doesn't have is a list of specific gifts for each and every person on the list. Instead, thrifty people buy gifts based on what they find on clearance. You might think that you can't get something that the recipient will love this way, but remember: you have the whole year to shop, since you made up your list really early.

Get out your list while you are standing in front of a 50% off or greater clearance rack and then start thinking, "Would Sally love those 80% off candlesticks? Would your dad love that 75% off drill bit set?"

Not having a set item list gives you the flexibility you need to give great gifts at a low cost.

Make a mental note throughout the year of what gifts really got used

This tip is mainly for people buying gifts for their children, but it works for other ages and stages as well.

Every Christmas, after my kids open their gifts, I place their gifts underneath the Christmas tree in a box. Two days after Christmas, I make a note of what gifts are still in the box. These types of gifts do not get bought again.

Later in the month I make a mental note of what gifts they are still playing with and which ones are now broken. The broken ones aren't bought again.

In the early years as a parent, doing these two things had me scaling down Christmas giving to my children year after year for quite a while. And the truth is that the children never once complained about receiving fewer gifts from us, because the ones they got were high quality and were what they really wanted.

As I said, this can also apply to more than just the gifts you give to your children. I have started applying this same principle to my husband and I. For instance, I note what gifts I received that I really did use all year long, and I put those on my gift list again. I also note which gifts made my husband's face light up versus which ones made him simply say a half-hearted "thanks."

This gift-giving step has saved us money, reduced household clutter, and increased gift satisfaction.

Decide if any activities need to be cut out of the Christmas budget, or at least reduced

Christmas tends to be a season of traditions, and that is something I do love about it; but here is the one thing I don't love about traditions — sometimes we continue them even though they don't make sense anymore.

Doing traditions the family has outgrown is a waste of money and time. After Christmas is over, gather everyone for a family meeting and ask each and every member what their favorite Christmas season activity was this year. Now ask them what was their least favorite.

The answers to these two questions may make you realize that everybody is really bored of that Christmas play you have been shelling out $100 for. You can choose to cut that $100 out of your Christmas budget altogether, or you can put it towards trying out a new Christmas activity next year. That choice is up to you, but to continue to spend it on the Christmas play is a waste of money; and thrifty people don't like to do that.

Our family recently evaluated our current family Christmas traditions. Our children are all teenagers or older now, and we discovered numerous traditions that the children really felt they had outgrown — and we had fun trying out new ones for this new stage of life. In the end our pocket book thanked us, and we enjoyed a more relaxing Christmas.

Snail-Pacing Action Step

There is a lot of information in this chapter, and I am sure those of you who are new to the thrifty lifestyle feel a bit overwhelmed. Please remember that you don't have to tackle this list all at one time. Pick the one thing I talked about in this chapter that you think will have the greatest impact on your family's Christmas budget and concentrate on doing it well this year. When you become efficient in that, then you can pick another.

Further Resources

I have written extensively on the topic of keeping the cost of Christmas low, and you can find links to those articles on the resource page for this book, which is at http://snailpacetransformations.com/thrifty-resources.

Thrifty People Know

WHEN THRIFTY EQUALS THRIVING

You have read what thrifty people are, what we do, and what we know; but you still might be thinking, "Why bother?"

Why bother living on less after the debts are paid? Yes, there is the easing of financial stress; yes, there is the ability to give to others; but is there more? When does the thriving happen?

Oh, yes, there is so much more. There is a whole world of opportunities that open up to you that would remain closed if you simply were thrifty until you got out of debt and then went back to spending every dollar you once paid to payments.

Here is our family's story of how years of thrifty living led to thriving. It really is very new. In fact, the major part of the story has yet to begin.

It began after my mom died. We had a choice: we could use her inheritance to get ourselves out of debt completely, or we could use it to make a pretty nice down payment on a grander home with a few acres. We chose the first and not the latter.

We faced this decision again when my maternal grandmother died, and then when my fraternal grandmother died — and once again when my father died.

Oh, we were tempted along the way! At one point, after my maternal grandmother died, we even did submit an offer on a steal-of-a-deal home. Ten acres and a home for $90,000. With the sale of our current home and the inheritance from her, we would have owned the home 100% debt free.

While waiting to hear if we qualified for a conventional mortgage that would help fill the gap between when we bought the new home and when we sold our current home, we started second-guessing ourselves. Sure, we would own the home outright as soon as our home sold, but it still did not solve our income problem.

In fact, it only made our income problem worse. There would be more property tax and more upkeep costs with a home with that much land. My husband already worked two jobs to pay our current bills for a small home in the city — and we had no debt.

When the bank called to say the conventional mortgage had been denied due to the extensive repairs the home needed, we considered it a closed door and did not push it any further.

On that day we began to see that the inheritance money we were receiving needed to be used to create another stream of income so that eventually we could afford both the cost of purchasing an acreage and the upkeep of it.

And that is what we did. So far we have purchased two rentals: one with inheritance money from my maternal grandmother, and one with inheritance money from my dad. We used the inheritance from my fraternal grandmother to fix up our first home and sell it, pay for two modest three-year-old vehicles, get the supplies I needed to start my blog, and create a three-month emergency fund.

As I said before, we did spend some of the money on a few memory-making family trips, but the bulk went into setting ourselves up for financial freedom.

With the second rental done, we had just enough money to to purchase a third rental if we found a really good deal; but we would need to save the money for the repairs.

We thought that was exactly what we would do, but then I began to have second thoughts. I began to think perhaps we really should make a trip back home to visit family. Perhaps we should start asking the neighbor of the ugly green home beside us if he would be willing to sell it so that we could take it down and thus have our property value go up.

My head was filled with possibilities our thrifty family never really had before; because all our various income streams plus our thrifty living practices were truly beginning to create something we never had before — margin.

WE HAD WIGGLE ROOM IN OUR BUDGET, AND WITH WIGGLE ROOM CAME SOMETHING AWESOME — CHOICES!

With many possibilities whirling in my head, I went in for what was supposed to be a routine mammogram. Two days later the clinic called; they saw something that needed further testing, but the next appointment wasn't until after the weekend.

The weekend was my birthday, so my family took me out both to celebrate and to get my mind off things. You see, my own mother had dealt with breast cancer. It wasn't the type of cancer that took her in the end, but it was the one that started her battle with several different cancers that eventually led to her death. So to say I was unsettled was an understatement.

While we were stopped at a gas station filling up for our day's adventure, I noticed a tiny RV and said to the kids, "Hey, that is the RV your dad and I want to get after you all leave the nest; we plan to tour the States and Canada in it."

They all turned to me and said, "If you get something bigger we will come with you; let's go now, Mom!" That entire day we started dreaming about doing the trip as a family. Eventually we got down to money. Could we really afford to do this?

I thought for sure the answer would be no, and the dream would stay just that — a dream. I was wrong. I realized if we took the last of the money from my dad, plus the money we were saving for a car (when we sell the RV at the end of the trip we will get this money back), and added in what we could save between then (March) and when we wanted to leave (January), plus what we would earn from the rentals and my blog while we were on the road, we could do it.

I ran the numbers a dozen different ways, and every way I ran them we could do it. I was shocked.

When I went in for the further testing early that next week, we were told that what they were seeing was nothing to be concerned about. (When I visited my doctor later, she said she believes that what I had was a cyclical breast cyst.)

After walking out of the clinic, my husband and I looked at each other and said, "So what now?" It took us about five seconds to decide that family time was precious and we should go for it.

Had we not continued to live thrifty even after we were 100% debt free, as well as continuing to create income streams from our windfalls, this road trip would not be a possibility.

In fact, if it were not for our thrifty lifestyle practices, we would not have been able to save what we needed from March until when we leave — just a few short weeks from when I am currently typing this.

To save the last of the money we needed, we have been reselling items like crazy, thus raising $5000. We have said "no" to a new dishwasher when ours broke.

When the upstairs bathroom developed a plumbing issue, we shut off water to it and are making do with the downstairs bathroom. We didn't want plumbing costs to steal from our trip fund.

EVERYONE HAS THE ABILITY TO GET TO THE POINT WHERE THEY HAVE WIGGLE ROOM IN THEIR BUDGETS.

I spent yard sale season looking for items we needed for the RV. We shopped clearance sales and thrift stores for other items. We purchased new when we had to, but when we did, we used thrifty practices to lower the price as much as possible.

On the road we will continue to use thrifty practices such as eating at our campsite six out of seven nights. We are purchasing a National Park pass to save entrance fees. We planned our route so that we could enjoy lower-priced and free activities like biking and hiking.

I know many will never receive an inheritance — let alone the numerous ones we have! — but I believe everyone has the ability to get to the point where they have wiggle room in their budgets. But they must be willing to embrace the thrifty lifestyle and generate income streams from their talents and windfalls.

There are numerous people with just one side job out there that earn more than our family does from my blog and our two rentals combined — and many cost very little to begin.

Our generation needs to stop thinking that a 9 to 5 job is all we need. The truth is that with the exception of a few professions, it rarely is. At least it isn't enough to keep us living like we like to live.

When you mix thrifty practices with creating more income streams, you can create financial margin — and with margin comes choices.

You have the ability to create financial surplus in your life. It comes with repeatedly making thrifty choice after thrifty choice, as well as thinking outside the box about how to use even the smallest financial windfalls to generate more income.

Further Resources

If following our trip will inspire you towards living a thrifty lifestyle and creating flexible income streams, I would love to have you do so at http://snailpacetransformations.com/rv-trip/.

Conclusion

Nonfiction books like this one are not meant to be like the majority of fiction books. You are not supposed to reach the last page and close the book and then that's it, the book is over, and it is time to grab another one off the shelf and enjoy escaping again.

No. Nonfiction books like this one are supposed to help you change your life. This one is supposed to help you change your finances in a positive way, which will in turn affect other aspects of your life.

Imagine what your life would be like if you didn't have to live in fear of a job loss, because you know you have a fully-stocked emergency fund that will get you through.

Or perhaps you can't imagine that, because it seems impossible, given where you are financially right now. If that is you, I challenge you to pick just one of these thrifty practices that you are not currently using and start doing it faithfully.

It might not give you that fully-funded emergency fund right away, but I bet you start to see a bit of wiggle room in the budget where previously it had none. Perhaps right now you are not even living within your budget. If that is the case, then these thrifty practices might first give you a budget that actually works — and then the wiggle room.

You are not financially stuck! You might feel that way, but there are things you can do to become unstuck. These things will take time to get used to; they require changing mindsets and habits, and that is hard stuff — but isn't shaking free of that stuck feeling worth it?

Perhaps you are one of the thrifty, lifelong learners who read this book to glean new thrifty principles. I hope you found at least one, and I hope you will start applying it.

There is always room for improvement in the life of a thrifty person.

I want to leave you with one last snail-pacing step. I want you to take the time to sit down this week, invite your significant other if you have one, and together think about what financial freedom looks like for you.

You don't have to write your ideas down on paper — unless you want to. Just discuss it enough so that you have a clear picture of what financial freedom would look like in your head, one that you can conjure up on those days when it is hard to make the right thrifty choice.

About the Author

Victoria is first and foremost a wife to Jack and a mom to Thomas, Aiden, and Courtney. Her main priority in life has been pursuing a successful launch of these four amazing products into the world. Well, okay, so really Jack's mom and dad launched him, and they did a pretty good job of it, too; but Victoria is the one that sends him out into that big world each day with a kiss and a smile.

Through her blog, *Snail Pace Transformations*, Victoria helps moms find the time and money they need to pursue their passions while maintaining balance in their lives. Not perfect balance, since that is nothing but a myth, but priority-based balance.

In her own life this has meant that often things beyond the day-to-day of raising a family get done at a slow snail-pacing rate, and she is okay with that. The speed at which success is gathered isn't what matters most; what matters most is that when we get to whatever finish line we are shooting for, we don't look back and realize we lost our most important priorities along the way.

Victoria's personal passions include running, biking, knitting, and coffee drinking. She has a huge love for dark chocolate and an obsession for renovation shows on TV.

Get To Know Victoria

Blog
http://snailpacetransformations.com

Facebook
https://www.facebook.com/snailpacetransformations

Instagram
SnailPaceTransformations

Twitter
@SnailPaceTrans

Pinterest
https://www.pinterest.com/snailpace/

Email
snailpacetransformations at gmail dot com

Weekly Newsletter
Sign up at
http://snailpacetransformations.com/thrifty-resources

Made in the USA
Las Vegas, NV
10 January 2021